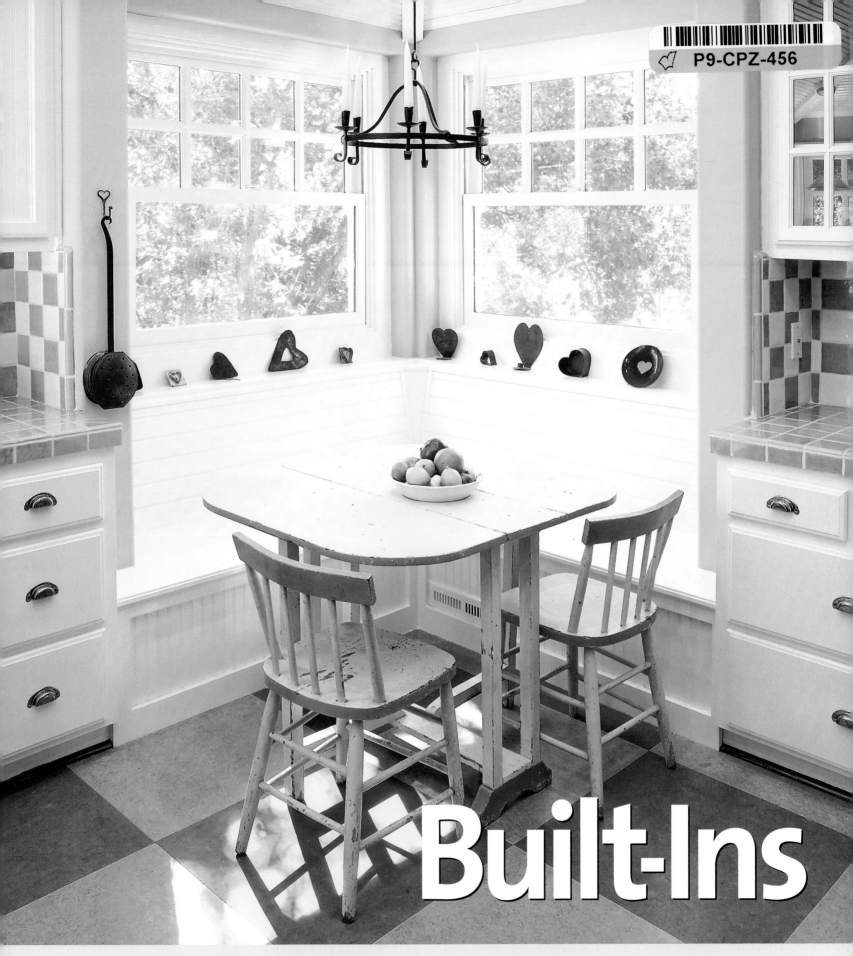

Built-Ins

by Jeanne Huber and the Editors of Sunset Books, Menlo Park, California

contents

Sunset Books

VP, EDITORIAL DIRECTOR
Bob Doyle

ART DIRECTOR
Vasken Guiragossian

Staff for This Book

MANAGING EDITOR
Ben Marks

DESIGNER
Susan Paris

COPY EDITOR
John Edmonds

PRINCIPAL PHOTOGRAPHER
Chuck Kuhn

PRINCIPAL ILLUSTRATOR
Greg Maxson

PROOFREADER
Pamela Cornelison

INDEXER
Marjorie Joy

PREPRESS COORDINATOR
Eligio Hernández

PRODUCTION SPECIALISTS
Linda M. Bouchard
Janie Farn

FRONT COVER PHOTOGRAPH
Photography by Jupiter Images.

For additional copies of *Built-Ins* or any other
Sunset book, visit us at www.sunsetbooks.com.

For more exciting home and garden ideas, visit

myhomeîdeas.com

the beauty of built-ins

THE TRICK TO CREATING A BEAUTIFUL BUILT-IN
IS THE ABILITY TO IDENTIFY THE ONES YOU MAY
ALREADY BE LIVING WITH. IN THIS CHAPTER, WE
HELP YOU SEE THE BONES BENEATH A BUILT-IN'S
FINISHED SURFACE SO YOU CAN CREATE YOUR
OWN ROOM DIVIDERS, WINDOW SEATS, BREAK-
FAST NOOKS, NICHES, DESKS, BOOKCASES, AND
SHELVES.

BUILT-IN ASSETS

SOME BUILT-INS ARE ATTACHED TO WALLS, while others are planted in the middle of a room or tucked into walls. They become part of the house in a way that movable furniture does not. Many advantages derive from this. Built-ins tucked under the eaves of a house or into a hallway wall, for example, take advantage of otherwise unused space. Other built-ins get some of their required strength from the wall they're attached to, so they have a more streamlined design. The table of a breakfast nook can be attached to the wall on one end so that it needs only a single leg on the other, saving enough space to allow four people to sit comfortably where a freestanding table of roughly the same size would accommodate only two. Built-ins also make cleaning a breeze, as dust bunnies can't hide under or behind a built-in bed or cabinet. Built-ins reduce visual clutter, help set a home's style, and add to its long-term value.

BELOW, RIGHT: Built-ins are often recessed into walls, a setup that takes advantage of space between studs and frees up floor space. You can even tuck shelves into curved walls.

BELOW: Sized to fit between a wall and a post, a small desk creates a sunny workspace that's perfect for keeping up with e-mail. A register for the heating and air-conditioning system fits into the base.

ABOVE, LEFT: Cozy spaces are perfect places to curl up with a good book. Windows on the nook's left wall brighten the partially enclosed space; drawers below provide storage.

ABOVE, RIGHT: Because built-ins are often crafted specifically for the places they fit, designs aren't limited to those you find in stores and catalogs. A custom, angled front panel adds perspective to this china cabinet.

A built-in handrail helps give this bookcase its custom-crafted look. On the landing, a simple built-in desk sits before a window, as if inviting people to pause and enjoy the view.

Building in details

Because built-ins are designed to fit specific spaces and serve individual needs, they often incorporate custom features. Sometimes these features play up architectural elements of the house and help define it as Craftsman or Colonial or modern. Custom features can also solve practical problems, such as making use of awkward spaces or squeezing a guest bed and an office into a room that also must serve as a family room. And custom features often exist to support personal hobbies or interests.

Creating a blackboard built into the back of a breakfast nook is easy. Just coat inexpensive, ultra-smooth hardboard with multiple layers of blackboard paint.

BELOW: A bookcase added to the end of a kitchen island anchors the dog's food and water bowls. Holes cut into the bottom shelf keep the bowls in place.

BOTTOM: You can create a lounging area for pets by removing the doors from a standard cabinet.

A high shelf with built-in lighting punches up the architectural impact of an otherwise simple bookcase. The shelf also solves a major design issue in this room: how to keep the fireplace from overwhelming the space. And by creating a sort of mini-ceiling, it makes this high-ceiling room seem more human-scale.

Recessed into a wall, a built-in cabinet (above, left) keeps bathroom towels handy and dry. A partial wall near a back door (above) appears to be topped by a wide, thick piece of molding. But those in the know lift the lid and find compartments for keys, parking meter money, and a cell phone charger.

Built-ins equip a front entry with all the essentials: hooks for jackets; a place to sit for putting on boots; and little drawers for keys, spare change, and other necessities.

The 4-by-8-foot slab of granite for the countertop was a bargain-priced off-color reject at a stone fabricator's shop.

On the dining room side, deep cabinets hold table linens and large serving dishes.

Plywood drawer fronts, doors, and end panels are pre-finished in bright yellow.

SEEING THE KEY COMPONENTS

BUILT-INS MAY LOOK COMPLEX, but at heart they're usually simple and unassuming. Most consist primarily of basic boxes containing shelves or drawers, which are essentially just smaller boxes. Underneath, there's usually a sturdy base. And alongside the boxes or between them, there are often filler strips or molding to tie the components together and make them fit precisely into the available space. Once you can mentally picture the components that go into built-ins, you'll be in a better position to design the features you want.

Homeowner Mike Muscardini sketched out a plan for a built-in cabinet that would double as a room divider between the living room and a slightly elevated dining room. For several thousand dollars, his hybrid approach resulted in a cabinet that he figures might have cost five times as much if he had simply ordered it custom-made.

Anatomy of a Room Divider

This room-divider cabinet consists essentially of six boxes, all made of inexpensive particleboard, plus a base, two end caps, and a countertop. The living room side is a foot taller than the dining room side, so the cabinet assembly steps up to match the elevation change between the rooms.

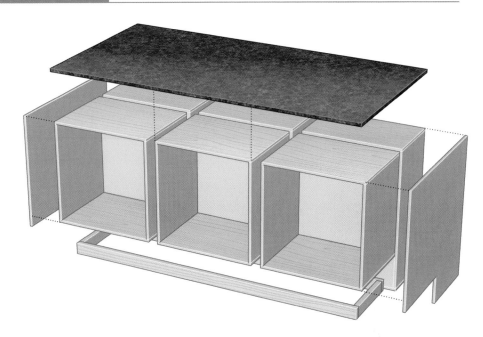

The interior of the built-in's particleboard boxes are covered with black melamine.

The living-room side of the divider functions as a bookcase.

The living room is two steps lower than the dining room.

WINDOW SEATS

SOME BUILT-INS EVOLVE FROM VERY SPECIFIC NEEDS—a way to tame the clutter of shoes and backpacks by the back door, for example, or a way to corral business and personal papers so that bills get paid on time. Others turn a house into a home. Window seats are perhaps the quintessential example of this sort of built-in. Yes, they add seating, but their main purpose usually is to cozy up a space.

Molding wraps up the legs and across the front of this window seat, creating a clean, modern look that's in keeping with other elements of the room's design.

A Shelf-Type Window Seat

A shelf-type window seat rests on 2 by 4 ledgers screwed to wall studs and a 2 by 4 across the front. For added strength, add bracing between the ledgers and the front, and attach 2 by 6 uprights at the ends. You could also add a leg at the center or install a front panel that reaches to the floor, as shown in the project on page 176–179. If you want wainscot above the seat, add nail strips to the walls first, as needed.

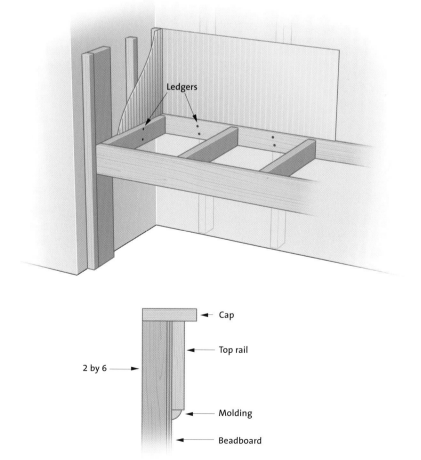

Ledgers

Cap

Top rail

2 by 6

Molding

Beadboard

Box-Style Window Seats

To create a window seat with an enclosed base, you can add a front panel to a shelf-type window seat or take an entirely different approach: Build one or more boxes and set them on a 2 × 4 or 2 × 6 base. You then have numerous options for detailing the front and its connection to walls on each side.

LEFT: With a baseboard to match that in the rest of the room, and a few trim pieces that mimic the look of frame-and-panel doors, this window seat looks more like furniture.

BELOW, LEFT: Bookcases frame this window seat, and there is matching trim on the surfaces around it. These features make the space seem more like a part of the house rather than just furniture. The connection between books and window seat also underscores the point that this is a great place to read.

BELOW, RIGHT: Another option is to build a window seat flush with whatever walls, cabinets, or closets are on the sides. Paint the surfaces in a way that links them, so they look like part of a single plan rather than separate elements.

Storage below window seats

Although some window seats have hinged tops that lift up to reveal storage underneath, it's also possible to add shelves or drawers that open on the front. While the concept is appealing, in practice it's tricky to do well. The biggest challenge is providing the storage space in a way that doesn't cause the window seat to become too high for comfort. Awkward window seats tend to become just places where clutter collects.

Architects generally recommend that window seats be no higher than 18 inches, including the cushion. If a room has tall baseboards that extend across the front of a window seat, standard 12-inch-tall cabinet boxes create a seat that's too high once you include cushions. But there are strategies for getting around this predicament.

Cubbies are one of the least expensive ways to incorporate storage in a window seat. You just build boxes open on one side and set them on a base with the opening facing into the room, then top them with a seat that spans the boxes. If you want a tall baseboard, the cubbies will have to be extra short, so consider making them wider. Two wide cubbies under this window seat work much better than three or four narrower compartments would.

RIGHT, TOP: **To create a window seat that follows a gentle curve, place a series of boxes side by side so their fronts match the bend. Adjust them so any gaps at the front are approximately equal, and use filler strips to cover these.**

RIGHT: **Two boxes set at right angles to each other create an L-shape window seat. Rather than extend one box all the way to the corner, which would create a dark hole that's difficult to access, set the boxes so the right side of one touches the left side of the other at the bend. This will close off the awkward corner space. If you don't want to sacrifice the space, install a pull-up door in the corner, under the cushion, as shown on page 179.**

Installing Upright Supports

Baskets that rest directly on the floor are a simpler option than drawers. They also make better use of the vertical space, allowing the window seat to be set lower. Dividers between the baskets keep them arranged in a tidy row. The dividers also support the window seat and help keep it from sagging.

Upright stabilized with dowels

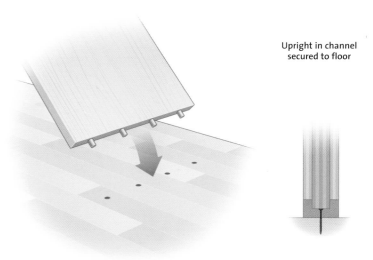

Upright in channel secured to floor

A relatively tall drawer fits under a window seat when the trim by the floor is thin. This may require you to switch to a different style of trim than the nearby baseboard.

A window seat with a short toekick looks visually balanced when the gap under the drawers matches the height of the trim piece that runs as a lip below the front of the cushions.

FINDING PLACES FOR BUILT-INS

BUILT-INS USUALLY SIT ALONGSIDE WALLS, but sometimes the connection is even closer. They may be tucked into the wall structure itself, or they might function as walls themselves.

Tucked-in options range from simple niches with just a shelf or two to entire cabinets with multiple drawers. Recessing built-ins all the way or only partially into walls maximizes storage space and minimizes clutter by keeping floor space open for other uses. And in many cases, it adds considerable charm to a home.

Recessing a cabinet into a wall

Walls framed with 2 × 4s or 2 × 6s have enough space between the studs to store CDs, videocassettes, DVDs, paperback books, and many collectibles. If you need deeper shelves, consider recessing them partway and letting the fronts extend into the room. The few extra inches you gain by using the stud space may make all the difference between adequate storage and shelving that's too shallow. Recessed cabinets work best in interior walls, where they don't compromise insulation. They're easiest to build in walls that are not load-bearing, meaning they don't support the weight of a floor or roof above. For complete instructions, see pages 192–195.

TOP: **Inset shelves like these fit between studs. Because the shower wall is wider than a person can easily reach across, the shelves extend only about halfway into the available space, which means similar shelves could be added to the adjoining room. Setting the shelves back a bit from the shower wall creates space for the plumbing.**

LEFT: **Recessed into a thick wall that doubles as a room divider, a built-in cabinet hides kitchen mess from diners' view and provides easy-to-use storage space. The top has two sets of shallow shelves, each accessible from one side. The deep cabinet on the bottom opens only from the dining room.**

Niches with only a subtle curve look more modern and provide more storage or display space on the top shelf.

Although it's possible to enclose a curved niche with a door that's round on top, it's much simpler to leave the top shelf as an open display area. Standard rectangular doors then fit below.

Building a Drywall Niche

Built-in niches add warmth and personality to a home. To create a niche curved on top, look for easy-to-install plastic inserts (see Resources, page 222) or create your own custom shape from a few pieces of plywood, scraps of wood, and drywall.

For the arch, use two layers of $^1/_4$-inch bending drywall, such as High Flex®, which can bend to a radius as small as 20 inches when dry or 14 inches if dampened on both sides. Or use standard $^1/_2$-inch drywall and score the back every $^1/_2$ to 1 inch, depending on the curve.

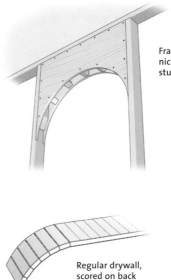

Frame for curved niche between studs

Regular drywall, scored on back

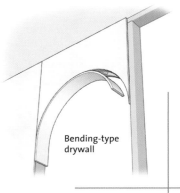

Bending-type drywall

RIGHT: Window seats take advantage of the space created by dormers in this upstairs hallway, and a shallow bookshelf bridges the gap between them. Outfitting a wide hallway with built-ins turns it from a mere passageway into an appealing, usable room.

Under eaves, behind knee walls

When a room is tucked underneath a slanted roof, the triangular space along the side of the room often goes unused. Even if it is covered by a low knee wall, this is a great place for built-in shelves, drawers, or a desk.

Knee walls rarely carry a structural load, so you can usually open up even a fairly large area without having to add headers or bracing. A structural engineer or experienced builder can confirm whether this is true in your house. If there is an access door in the knee wall, crawl inside and check for wiring before you settle on a plan. If the space behind the knee wall is deep and you're building shallow shelves, include an access door so you can still use the remaining space for storage.

ABOVE: Depending on the situation, built-ins that take advantage of space under the eaves can open on the side or front— or both.

Shelves built into knee walls can be boxed in on top (far left), or they can be set into angled cabinets to take more advantage of the available space (left). You can leave the angled space open or outfit it with a shelf that isn't as deep as the others. It's also possible to create storage space for boxes, skis, or other bulky items behind a knee wall while still using some of the space for a built-in that opens directly into the room. In these rooms, the access doors are designed to go with their adjacent built-in cabinets.

Adding a Built-In Desk

Though it's possible to build an opening in a knee wall much as you'd frame and insulate a standard wall, it's usually easier to insert a plywood box with insulation already attached. In most cases, the box doubles as the shell of the built-in. In this example, it's the case for the top of the desk.

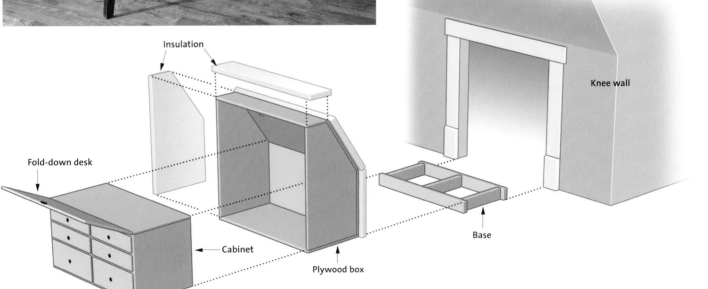

To recess a desk into a knee wall, cut a small opening and determine the available space and roof angle. Widen the opening after you find a bureau that fits with at least 4 inches to spare in each direction. Build a 3/4-inch-thick plywood box, using hardwood plywood so the top portion has a finished look. Attach rigid foam insulation, and caulk joints before you slide the box into place on a 2-by-4 base that has insulation in the spaces. Caulk joints on the front before you slide in the bureau. Screw it in place, then add details such as the fold-down desktop and molding.

Using space around the stairs

Stairways are great places for built-ins. You can add storage to the triangular spaces under stairways, as well as to the walls alongside steps and on landings. Bookshelves, drawers, benches, cubbies, and desks all make great use of these otherwise unused spaces, and the intriguing angles often make even simple features look stunning.

Because most stairways are wider than a person can easily reach across, you'll need a strategy to ensure that storage underneath isn't too deep to use efficiently. There are numerous options: Recess the built-in, making the space more like a nook. Build relatively shallow cabinet boxes and forget using the space behind them. Add half-depth built-ins under both sides of the staircase. Build pantry-style pullout drawers that you access from the sides. Or create a built-in that tucks under the stairs as if it were under an eave.

ABOVE: **Backpacks and other gear typically dropped by the door find a home in under-stairs cubbies. These cubbies are flush with the side of the stairs but closed in on the back, keeping the overall depth reasonable. Cubbies 18 inches deep are easy to use, though they can reach back to 24 inches.**

LEFT: **Stairways that turn at a landing provide three distinct opportunities for built-ins. Here, window seats have been installed both below and on the landing itself. Where the stairs rise past the landing, there's enough headroom for a closet.**

Angled Shelf Supports

There's enough space under the bottom flight of stairs for shallow shelves plus a desk and chair.

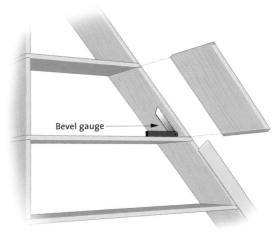

Bevel gauge

Use a bevel gauge to determine the angle at which the stairs rise. Then set a table saw, jigsaw, or compound miter saw blade to that angle and cut the boards to length. The angles on the ends of the shelf boards and the supports are the same.

No space goes to waste in this arrangement. The shelves are recessed under the stairs, which adds a spacious feeling to the room and ensures that the cubbies don't become so deep that things become lost in them.

Stacked boxes that hide under stairs

OPPOSITE: Open shelves march up this stairway at the rate of one shelf per two treads. Beyond easy reach, the spaces are closed off with boards. A combination of drawers and cabinets with doors makes efficient use of the under-stairs space.

BELOW: This built-in storage system evokes the look of Japanese *tansu*, thanks to its combination of dark and light woods, black hardware, and different sizes of doors and drawers.

Because of the angles in a stairway, it can be hard to envision the best way to use the space underneath. But if you approach the task as though you were a child stacking blocks or boxes, it suddenly becomes easier. Divide the space into rectangular areas and fit key components into those. Leave the remaining small triangular spaces as cubbies, or cover them with paneling or doors cut at an angle.

You'll be following in the architectural tradition of Japan. Traditional homes there use *tansu*, or chests, for storage. One kind, called *kaidan-dansu*, or step chests, once doubled as storage units and steps to an upper elevation. When word got out that the taxman was coming, the chests were quickly rearranged to become storage alone, effectively erasing the upper space from what could be assessed. Traditional step chests are made in modular sizes, so two short chests, for example, can be paired with one tall one to create steps of equal height. It's a good strategy to use in planning modern built-ins under stairs, too.

Hidden Treasures

This stairway appears to have a closet at the end and paneling underneath. Press on side panels, though, and doors pop open to reveal deep drawers on full-extension slides. Magnetic spring latches eliminate the need for handles.

Using built-ins as room dividers

Open floor plans are great, up to a point. Activities naturally spill over from one space to the next, so there's less tendency for people to bunch up in one space while leaving other rooms empty. But too much openness can also have drawbacks. When dining and food preparation occur in one room, all the mess is on display when you sit down to eat. When a family room and an office are one, there may be too much commotion to get any work done.

With a built-in that doubles as a room divider, you may find a happy compromise. It can define and partially separate spaces yet not completely close one off. Plus, you get the benefit of whatever storage or other useful features are incorporated in the divider.

A combination tub surround, vanity and mirror wall serves as a centerpiece in a bathroom. This type of built-in would function especially well in an en suite bathroom, which has no wall separating it from a bedroom.

RIGHT: Built-in upper and lower cabinets make a kitchen and dining room seem like separate rooms. But the spaces remain well connected, thanks to the wide opening in the middle, the open spaces under the upper cabinets, and the use of glass doors on both sides of the upper cabinets.

DESIGN TIP

If you are using upper and lower cabinets to separate a kitchen from a dining room or living room, raise the upper cabinets above eye level if you want to encourage conversation between the rooms. Lower them if you are more interested in hiding kitchen mess from diners. Avoid hanging cabinets so the bottom shelf is at eye level, which is irritating and doesn't serve either practical purpose.

An otherwise wide-open space in this house is divided by built-ins that form a cube. Glass shelves face the dining room side (left). Around the corners, there are doors on both sides. One leads to a bathroom in the center, the other to a pantry. The far side of the cube contains a compact office (above), which is equipped with sliding doors that ensure quiet even when there's hubbub in surrounding spaces.

A simple built-in shelf installed along the ceiling provides good psychological separation for a kitchen, yet it doesn't intrude on the spacious opening between it and the adjoining room. The shelf echoes the detailing above cabinets on the far wall.

ABOVE: Adding doors to sections of this wall unit make it look more substantial and built in.

RIGHT: Two tall bookcases take on the look of a wall system when vertical dividers link some of the shelves. Molding connects the shelf units to the fireplace surround.

Fitting built-ins along a wall

Creating a built-in that spans an entire wall might seem an intimidating task. The trick is to divide it into manageable sections. Most wall systems are essentially just a stack of boxes set on a sturdy base. Some consist of a series of shelves or cabinets attached to the wall.

Symmetrical designs usually please the eye. Asymmetrical arrangements can too, as long as they are balanced. If you want one large opening to display artwork, for example, pair it with several small openings filled with other art objects. Or balance the design diagonally by using a large door on one side to visually anchor a large opening at the top on the other side.

In some situations, an entire wall of built-ins can overwhelm a room. Varying cabinet depth and trim detail makes a large array seem less intimidating.

A Wall of Boxes

This symmetrical wall system is essentially just 13 boxes stacked on a sturdy base. Note that the boxes in the top row are not as deep as those below. In a setup like this, it's important to leave a little wiggle room—at least an inch—between the end cabinets and the walls. That provides clearance so the doors open and allows you to custom-shape a filler strip to disguise any unevenness in the wall.

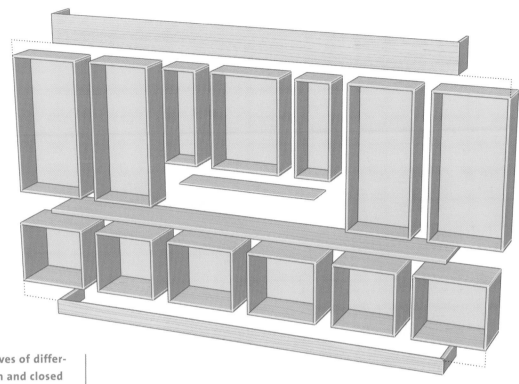

Though this wall system contains shelves of different widths and depths, as well as open and closed base cabinets, it's visually balanced because the elements are arranged in a symmetrical pattern.

HOW TO USE COLOR

AS YOU DESIGN BUILT-INS FOR YOUR HOME, also consider the effects of whatever finishes you will eventually apply. Clear finishes on dark wood, clear finishes on light wood, and paint all have very different effects.

Paint involves the most complex issues because color is a magic wand for built-ins. Shelves or cabinets almost disappear when painted a neutral color, especially where the walls and ceiling are a similar shade. This fact is worth remembering if you like the current look of a room but need to add storage space or fit in an office or spare bed. Coat built-ins in a vivid color, though, and they become stars of the room. It's an easy way to spark up a dull space. Neither option is intrinsically better or worse than the other. It all depends on the mood you are trying to create.

If you design a built-in with some traditional features but want to make it clearly a mod-ern interpretation, choosing a nontraditional color makes your point clear. This neo-Colonial fireplace wall might look like a poor cousin of a true antique if it had a natural wood finish. Bright paint makes it fresh and creative.

ABOVE: If you're adding simple bookcases, painting them a striking color is an easy way to give them dramatic effect. The purple paint in this room plays off the bright colors of the upholstery and carpet.

BELOW: Varying the surface treatments on built-ins changes their impact. In this dining room, the china cabinet stands out because of its natural wood look, while the cabinets on each side blend in with the walls and ceiling.

White paint on built-ins juxtaposed with wall paint that contains a whisper of yellow creates a serene backdrop for this living room. Painting walls and built-ins the same or similar shades, especially in subdued colors, deemphasizes the cabinets and makes them seem almost like ordinary wall surfaces.

Color for architectural effect

You can play up or tone down certain architectural features of built-ins simply by how you use color. Intricate moldings, for example, become much more noticeable if they are a different color than the background surface.

Another trick: If you want to emphasize what's in a display cabinet, paint the trim around it a different color than the cabinet interior or the nearby walls. The paint will turn the trim into the equivalent of a picture frame and draw the eye toward what's inside.

You can also use different shades or tints of a single color to good effect. If you paint walls one color and then choose a slightly darker color for the interior of an open cabinet on that wall, the cabinet will seem several inches deeper than it really is. This illusion, in turn, will make the room seem slightly larger. It will also make the cabinet more prominent.

ABOVE: Painting the interior of a cabinet a darker shade than a nearby wall creates the illusion of shadows. Pristine white woodwork heightens the contrast.

LEFT: With paint alone, you can mimic the look of elaborate molding. Carrying out this sleight of hand takes a lot of skill, but more freeform design, like the one in this pantry, can be just as effective.

To Harmonize or Contrast?

Regardless of the actual textures involved, color plays a huge role in determining whether built-ins appear to be elegantly simple or classically ornate. This room (below, left) has numerous fancy features, including built-ins with clamshell tops. But the monochrome paint scheme subdues the effect. With trim painted in a lighter shade than the walls, built-ins in this room (bottom) seem far more elaborate. Painting molding or recessed areas a darker color (below, right) pumps up the contrast even more.

Mixing it up

Spot use of color adds flair and energy to bookcases, cabinets, and other built-ins. A color wheel (right) helps you choose combinations that work well.

For a quiet, restful look Stay with one basic color or hue, but detail some surfaces by mixing the paint with a little white (to make what in color lingo is known as a tint) or black (to create a shade), or even some of the opposite color (for a complement tint).

For a slightly livelier look Go with an analogous color scheme: three colors that are side by side on a color wheel but have the same amount of black or white.

For maximum punch Pick complementary colors, which are opposites on a color wheel, or try variations such as split complementary colors (one color plus those on each side of its complement) or double-split complementary colors (the four colors that are on either side of a pair of complementary colors).

Shade

Hue

Tint

Complement tint

RIGHT: **A simple bookcase serves almost like a piece of artwork when each section is painted a distinct color. Detailing each section separately creates the look of display cubes, rather than basic shelves.**

BUILDING TIP

It's a bit tricky to create sections of different colors in a built-in with moveable shelves. Any drips will show as dried paint globs should you ever adjust the spacing. An easy solution if you want the colors only at the back: Use fabric-covered inserts. Cut foam-core board to fit, fold slightly oversize fabric over it, and glue the excess fabric to the back.

RIGHT: An entryway and kitchen built-ins owe most of their style to the paint colors. Though the color selection is unconventional, it's evident that a lot of thought went into choosing which color to use where. The panels next to the stairs match the door panels, and the stair treads pick up the color of the door. Green bands pull the colors together.

BELOW: Bright colors on the interior of a built-in add sparkle but aren't too flashy, since the books and other objects on the shelves create their own random compositions.

ABOVE: There's something delightful about opening up a cabinet and finding a contrasting color inside. If you add a lamp that's directly under a shelf, use a compact-fluorescent bulb, which stays cool, so you don't create a fire hazard.

FINISHING TOUCHES

OF ALL THE WAYS TO EMBELLISH BUILT-INS to make them more useful and stylish, adding doors is one of the most effective. Doors boost the architectural statement that a built-in makes. They are usually the biggest feature, so their style sets the tone of the overall piece. Doors also make it easier to keep items inside a built-in clean, as dust can't get in as easily.

Adding doors to a built-in may create one complication, though. Assuming you install standard doors, you'll need to leave free space in front, or the doors won't be able to swing open. If you don't have room for that, consider other types of doors.

The doors give this buffet a Craftsman look. Though the absence of visible hinges hints that it's a modern piece, the door style harkens back to the days when doors were made of solid wood rather than plywood or particle-board.

Tambour doors roll up. Kitchen cabinet companies sell kits that are easy to assemble.

Lift-up doors (above), which require special hinge mechanisms, don't intrude on the space in front when they are open, but they do temporarily block access to the cabinet above. Doors can also swing down, as these do (right).

Window shades (left) are perhaps the simplest kind of "door." They work well when your main goal is to keep out dust or sunlight, which can cause colors to fade.

Bifold doors (left) consist of two panels hinged side by side. Because they fold at the middle, they require less swing space than standard doors. To minimize swing space even more, bifold doors are often joined to the cabinet box with pocket-door hinges, which allow the doors to slide into the case at the sides. Equipped that way, the doors are often called flipper doors and are common features on entertainment centers.

Multi-purpose doors

While all doors on built-ins help define the style of a piece, some
doors do even more. Here are two doors that pile on the functionality.

Sliding doors coated with multiple layers of blackboard paint enclose a washer
and dryer, as well as the built-in cabinets that help one wall of this kitchen
function as a laundry room. Besides serving the practical purpose of shielding
these appliances from view, the doors provide a place for notes and lists, and
they keep kids entertained when parents are busy with meal preparation.

This built-in (top left) appears to be a traditional corner cabinet with elaborately detailed glass doors. But the visible part is actually a wider, deeper
door that swings open on concealed pivot hinges to reveal a hidden compart-
ment behind (bottom left). Companies that specialize in bookshelf doors
(see Resources) make simple-appearing shelf units that swing or slide open
to reveal hidden rooms or additional storage space behind.

Shelves usually work fine in upper cabinets, which tend to be relatively shallow. But deeper base cabinets benefit from drawers. A cabinet with glass doors on top and drawers on the bottom makes a classic built-in china cabinet.

Beaded molding around drawer openings gives a built-in cabinet the look of fine antique furniture.

Drawers and shelves

Drawers allow built-ins to store items where they are out of sight yet easily accessible, even in deep cabinets. This is one reason that kitchen designers increasingly urge people to specify drawers, not shelves, for base cabinets, which are typically 2 feet deep.

Sliding shelves behave like drawers but hide behind doors when not in use. They have low sides, making them less useful for storing numerous small items but perfect for pieces that don't tip, such as pots and pans. Because the sides don't fill all of the space vertically, you can adjust the spacing, just as you might a shelf, if your needs change. For example, in an entertainment center, you could use the flexibility of sliding shelves to adjust the spacing in a cabinet to suit a new generation of media products.

Drawers work well in base cabinets because you can peer down to inspect the contents. If you want to keep small or personal items on upper shelves, bins and baskets are good substitutes for drawers. You can take down the containers to get at what's inside.

Adding molding

On built-ins, strips of molding work like ribbons on a package: They tie parts together and add a decorative touch. Moldings fill gaps between cabinet sections and make them appear to be one. They also disguise edges of plywood or particleboard, and they dress up simple components. Molding plays a big role in defining the style of a piece—often a key to making a built-in look like it belongs in a specific house. Moldings come in simple shapes befitting Shaker, Craftsman, or modern homes, as well as in more ornate designs that help create Baroque or Victorian styles.

ABOVE: Crown molding with dentil detail—named because it resembles teeth—rings the top of these built-in cabinets. The carved design on the fireplace is an overlay molding, meaning it is glued on and not carved from the background wood.

RIGHT: To fit well in a room with a beamed ceiling, this wall system has Tudor touches. The top trim is known as label molding, traditionally used on the exterior of Tudor buildings to divert rainwater away from a doorway or window. The triangular shape over the main display area is a stripped-down version of a Tudor arch.

Decorative molding with a carved or pressed-in design can make a big fashion statement. Here, just a few pieces of expensive molding in a pierced agapanthus design go a long way toward establishing an ornate look. Other trim pieces are simpler.

Trim makes all the difference in determining whether cabinets look built into or pasted onto a room. In this bedroom, the seamless built-in look results from the cabinet's crown molding and perimeter casing being carefully matched to the moldings used elsewhere in the room.

Simple molding often works best. Here, it covers places where separate cabinet boxes meet, and bridges gaps between the cabinets and the walls. Painted white, the plain molding helps the built-in bookcase seem almost as airy as the small-pane windows in the doors and the bay window beyond.

Choose feet for a furniture look

Although built-ins are often designed to appear like part of a room's structure, there are times when they look better as furniture. If you want cabinets and bookcases to look lighter and more stylish, set them on legs or feet rather than on the usual toe-kick base. In a room with numerous built-ins, giving some components this treatment makes the overall effect less overwhelming. It also adds welcome variety and helps establish a distinctive style.

Possibilities for legs or feet range from elaborately carved or turned wooden pieces to sleek metal posts. Built-ins can rest on these, or they can be set on bases that have feet attached to the front as purely decorative trim. There are practical issues involved in the choice of whether to add true feet or pretenders backed up by a solid base. You'll need to clean under cabinets that sit on legs but not those on bases. However, if a heat register happens to lie under or behind the cabinet, you'll need to build in a vent or reroute the ducting if you want a solid base. With true legs or feet, a cabinet doesn't block airflow.

Satin-finished chrome legs almost disappear, making this island built-in seem to float. The L-shaped room divider contains a closet on the back, behind the headboard. That converts part of the spacious master bedroom into a dressing area and increases privacy in the sleeping area. Visible from the side are a high closet and a bureau.

Furniture legs that are turned on a lathe work as faux feet for built-ins that sit on a solid base.

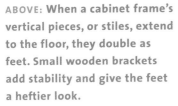

ABOVE: When a cabinet frame's vertical pieces, or stiles, extend to the floor, they double as feet. Small wooden brackets add stability and give the feet a heftier look.

ABOVE, LEFT: In this bathroom, sink cabinets appear to rest on legs, while drawer units sit firmly on solid bases. In reality, though, a solid base runs under all of the cabinets, and baseboard trim juts in and out to accommodate the different depths. Trimming baseboard in this way is one approach to creating the look of legs on cabinets.

ABOVE, RIGHT: Modified plinth blocks, traditionally found at the base of columns, serve as mock feet on this built-in.

LEFT: Along with the horizontal wood grain, the stylish faucet and pulls, and the farmhouse sink, the brushed-nickel legs under this cabinet give this built-in its energy and excitement.

PLAYING WITH CURVES

IN A WORLD FILLED WITH RIGHT ANGLES, a curve or two really stands out. Road builders know this, as do baseball pitchers. Designers of built-ins benefit from this insight too. With a smooth circular or elliptical feature, or an S-shaped (or cyma) curve, a built-in instantly becomes more warm and personal. Niches with arched tops, shelves or counters supported by curved brackets, and cornices between cabinets are some of the places where curves work well. They usually take a little more time or money to create, but the investment is worth it. These features are likely to become some of the most loved details in a home.

BELOW: Brackets are the simplest way to add curved detail to a built-in. The large ones under the upper cabinets have a cyma recta curve—one that's S-shaped and bulges out at the bottom. The smaller brackets in the base cabinet have a cavetto curve—a concave semicircle.

With a few flourishes, a simple elliptical curve morphs into a glamorous, whimsical design, such as this front for a stove alcove.

Drawing a Smooth Ellipsis

A curved cornice gives an otherwise simple built-in desk a lot of charm. Creating a feature like this is relatively simple. Make a template showing an elliptical curve, build framing as shown in the illustration on page 17, and attach drywall that you've scored on the back so the piece conforms to the curve.

Two screws driven into the base of a template, a length of string, and a marker are all you need to lay out a perfect ellipsis for a curved feature, such as a cornice between cabinets or walls.

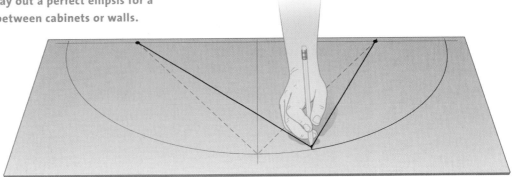

EMBELLISHING WITH BEADBOARD

BEFORE PLYWOOD BECAME WIDELY AVAILABLE, trim carpenters often turned to beadboard when they needed to create large panels for doors or to cover walls or ceilings. Milled with a tongue on one long edge and a mating groove on the other, beadboard pieces arrived from a lumberyard ready to be assembled into a relatively flat sheet—the only product available then with that feature. Today, we can choose from a wide array of panel products—including plywood, particleboard, and even plastic—that are shaped to resemble beadboard. The traditional kind of beadboard is still available as well.

Solid wood expands and contracts widthwise as humidity changes, so traditional beadboard is cleverly designed with a V groove, or bead, down the center as well as a beveled surface alongside the tongue and groove of each board. Mated together, the bevels create an additional V, which looks about the same regardless of whether the boards grow a little wider or shrink a bit. Were the boards designed to sit flush, any gap that opened up would be much more noticeable.

Traditional bead-board has deeper grooves than most of the panel products do, so it conveys an especially rich, historical look.

BELOW: **Beadboard plywood or MDF adds subtle decoration to an entryway built-in. The plywood version is less likely to chip if someone bangs it with a heavy object.**

ABOVE: Using beadboard behind open shelves adds interesting texture to a wall system.

LEFT: Beadboard gives a slightly antique look to a built-in china cabinet. Other details also help. They include the small-pane glass doors, the glass knobs, and the butler's tray prepped for high tea.

LEFT: Beadboard plywood or MDF makes a great center panel for frame-and-panel doors. Traditional beadboard made of solid wood can also be used this way.

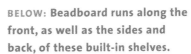

BELOW: Beadboard runs along the front, as well as the sides and back, of these built-in shelves.

DID YOU KNOW?

Beadboard has been used as wainscoting (a covering for the lower part of walls) since the Victorian era because wood stands up to dings better than plaster does. Since then, carpenters have used the material to panel entire walls and ceilings, especially in kitchens, hallways, dens, and porches, and in cabins and beach houses. Because of this rich tradition, the material adds a touch of history and the look of fine craftsmanship. The good news for do-it-yourselfers is that many of today's beadboard products are as easy to build with as any type of paneling.

USING LIGHT TO DECORATE

Careful planning makes it easier to incorporate lighting into built-ins. Here, the curved cornice and the thick walls on the bookcases provide space for wiring.

LIGHT ADDS MAGIC TO BUILT-IN CABINETS, especially those used for display or as room dividers. The light source can be on top, inside, underneath, or behind. Each has a different effect. The type of light also matters. Some possibilities are LEDs, fluorescents, and incandescents, including xenon-filled bulbs and low-voltage halogens. Standard halogens create too much heat to be used safely as cabinet lighting. The coolest and most energy-efficient options are LEDs and fluorescents. If you want to be able to dim the lights, though, incandescents are a common choice, though it's also possible to buy dimmable fluorescents.

- QUALITY OF LIGHT. Modern fluorescents with a color temperature of 3,000K or 3,500K duplicate the warm white light of incandescents. Halogens excel in delivering crisp light that makes many displays look almost as vivid as jewels. Daylight bulbs sound appealing, but their bluish light looks harsh in many applications.
- CABINET CHOICES. Look for lights in strips or ropes, which you can string out wherever you want, or attach with double-stick tape to surfaces such as the interior of a cabinet's face frame. Because they're easy to move, they are the best option in cabinets with adjustable shelves. Other lights are housed in discs as thin as ⅜ inch that you can attach to the underside of shelves. Fluorescent lights, available in fixtures as thin as 1 inch, are often used under or over cabinets.
- ABOUT FIXTURES. Some cabinet fixtures may specify that they can be used only with the bulb in one position—up or down. Select fixtures designed for upward use if you want to light the ceiling. Use downward-facing fixtures to illuminate countertops or objects on shelves.

Artificial light isn't the only way to illuminate cabinets. You can also locate cabinets so light from windows shines through open shelves or translucent doors.

When a cabinet is located in front of a window, painting the interior a vivid color enhances the effect because of the way the light bounces around.

ABOVE: To illuminate the interior of a cabinet, consider thin strips of LED lights. You can connect them and mount strips inside the face frame of the cabinet.

RIGHT: Accent lighting with a defined beam that casts hard shadows focuses attention on the objects you are displaying. For an effect like this, options include low-voltage halogen lamps called MR16s, as well as xenon-filled incandescent bulbs and LEDs.

ABOVE: Fluorescent bulbs are one of the best options for creating a band of light over a cabinet. To silhouette a display, like this, the bulbs should be placed near the wall. But to create indirect illumination in a room by bouncing light off a ceiling, place bulbs near the front. Allow at least 12 inches between the top of the cabinet and the ceiling, and paint the ceiling a light color.

built-ins for every room

FROM BEDROOM TO BATHROOMS, KITCHENS TO DINING ROOMS, BUILT-INS ADD COMFORT, STYLE, AND FUNCTIONALITY TO EVERY ROOM IN THE HOUSE. IN THIS CHAPTER WE SHOW YOU HOW BUILT-INS CAN TRANSFORM KITCHENS, ENHANCE HOME-ENTERTAINMENT AREAS, COZY-UP A LIVING ROOM, AND MAKE HOME OFFICES AS EFFICIENT AS POSSIBLE.

OUTFITTING LIVING ROOMS

IN SOME HOUSES, LIVING ROOMS SIT EMPTY most of the time, while in others they are filled with activity. People gather to watch TV or movies, listen to music, play games, or just sit by the fire and read. House layouts explain part of the difference, as do furnishings. Built-ins go a long way toward cozying up the space and equipping it for activities that make people want to linger.

Some of the built-in features that work best in living rooms include window seats, especially those with nearby storage for books or games; entertainment centers; display cabinets; and specialized storage for necessities such as firewood.

LEFT: **When a living room seems sterile, one sure cure is to put books or treasured collectibles on display. A comfortable chair and a good reading light are other essentials.**

BELOW: **Built-in cabinetry helps convert an oversize TV into the center-piece of a home theater setup. Today's big-screen plasma and liquid-crystal display, or LCD, digital televisions are so wide that they're rarely hidden behind cabinet doors.**

FAR RIGHT: A fireplace is the focal point in many living rooms. Built-ins on one or both sides keep a single element from stealing the show. The cabinets also make good use of space that's not a prime area for seating because it's too far back to have a view of the fire.

RIGHT: This built-in cabinet beside a fireplace was designed to look like an antique recessed into the wall of this Country French living room. The curtain-lined glass cabinet doors add to the look.

A built-in room divider shelters a seating area from hubbub in the rest of the space yet doesn't block the view or natural light. Bonus features include storage space and a countertop that's especially useful when the home-owners entertain.

Building in a TV

Televisions have changed a lot over the past few years. Many newer TVs have much wider screens but far thinner profiles. While not exactly light, flat-screen TVs are slender enough to be hung like pictures on a wall. The face dimensions of older screens were almost square because the old analog TV signals were broadcast to fit within a 4:3 ratio of width to height. But the TV industry now uses digital signals, which fit a wide-screen format with a 16:9 ratio. This makes televisions more horizontal, like movie screens.

For someone playing a video game or watching a movie, the wider screen is great because more of the action is in view. However, the new shape does pose issues if you want to hide the TV behind doors. Because the screen is so wide, swinging doors tend to take up too much space in the room. Pocket-style doors work, but the cabinet must be at least half as deep as the opening is wide, which isn't always possible. Other options include sliding doors, tambour doors, and doors that fold up on special hinges. Or you can do what many people are doing and just leave the TV in plain sight.

TOP: **Slightly recessing the TV and tucking it into a niche outfitted with drawers and shelves subtly minimizes its presence without significantly impacting views.**

ABOVE: **Most new televisions are thin enough to fit easily within the depth of standard bookshelves in built-in cabinets.**

LEFT: **In wall systems with deep shelves, you can bring the screen of a thin TV to the front by setting it into a face frame that's flush with other cabinet features.**

Hiding Flat Panels

More and more people are content to leave a TV in the open. But there are still situations in which you might want to disguise it. Here are a few options to consider.

Sliding doors create an either-or option. You have a choice of seeing the bookcases (left) or the TV (right). For this type of door, you need to have cabinets on both sides that are each at least half as wide as the TV. To keep sliding doors from looking too squat, make them taller than the TV.

Pocket-style doors have long been a favorite on entertainment centers because they tuck out of the way. But with the new, horizontal TVs, the geometry is occasionally challenging. Pocket-style doors work best on cabinets that are at least half as deep as the opening is wide. In this case, aesthetic considerations dictated that this cabinet/room divider (left) needed to be relatively shallow, so the homeowners had their flat-panel TV mounted to an arm that extends to let the TV clear the partially recessed doors (right).

Most of the time, this living room has a typical, classical look, with a fireplace topped by a mirror as its focal point (left). But a television is hidden in a recess behind the mirror, and the mirror is a two-way type. It becomes translucent when illuminated from behind (right). LCD and plasma TVs work well in a situation like this because of their slender profile.

Display niches and shelves with their own lights, as well as a fireplace, are built into this wall system, but its primary focus is clearly the TV. The main speaker, which delivers 80 percent of the sound, is right in the middle, where it belongs. Auxiliary speakers are on the sides. Other components fit into niches. There is plenty of storage space behind closed doors as well as on the open shelves. To create a finished look to the front, speakers hide behind fabric panels (below) secured to frames that match the cabinetry.

Sound considerations

If you house a TV in a built-in, try to locate the screen so the center will be at eye level when you watch, especially if you have a rear-projection model. Some screens look dim if you view them at an angle. Eye level for an adult sitting on a couch or chair is usually 38 to 42 inches from the floor. Digital signals have a finer dot pattern than the old analog signals did, so you can sit closer without noticing the individual dots. A screen that measures 30 inches across diagonally needs to be only 6 feet from you rather than 8. For larger TVs, add about 2 feet to the minimum viewing distance for each additional 10 inches of screen size. Among the other issues to consider as you plan built-ins:

Place the main speaker, which delivers spoken words, directly above or below the screen. The new TVs allow for six audio channels, but speech still needs to come primarily from the same direction as the screen or it will seem odd. If you can't place the main speaker at the front, at least point it toward you.

Provide vents to allow a steady airflow that will disperse the heat the equipment generates. Avoid stacking components directly on top of each other. Place them on separate shelves a few inches apart. If you have closed doors over the front of a cabinet, you need vents on the back and possibly louvers between shelves.

Add doors, if you wish, to cover DVD players, CD players, and other components, even if you have decided to leave the TV exposed. These other components are less than 18 inches wide, so standard doors work fine.

Besides building custom cabinets to house entertainment gear, you can instead purchase a ready-made case and insert it into a niche trimmed out to match the room. Look for a cabinet that swivels when you pull it out so that you can easily reach the back to change wiring.

SOUND TIP

If you don't have room for multiple speakers or don't want the complication of setting them up, consider designing your built-in to accommodate a sound bar. This low-profile box contains dozens of speakers that use psychoacoustics to mimic surround sound. The speakers deliver sounds at slightly different volume, frequency and timing, so they seem to come from different directions. Buy and try out the equipment before you commit to a built-in design, so you're sure to leave the right size opening.

For a large collection of CDs or other media, custom-size shelves or drawers make the most efficient use of space, and transform your collection into a veritable work of art.

A home for books

Bookcases are arguably the simplest and most useful kind of built-in. As you begin planning, think about the books are in your collection and what you intend to add over the years. The depth of shelves and the distance between supports are the most critical factors, as these can't be changed once a bookcase is built.

Determine the depth

by measuring the width of the largest books you plan to store upright or flat. Shelves should be a little deeper than the books, as recessed volumes don't collect as much dust. Though you may decide to store some large volumes flat, or use a few piles as bookends, you'll want to store most titles upright. In that position, books are easy to retrieve and put back, and you don't risk crushing the bindings.

A soffit rings this living room above the bookshelves, unifying the space and closing off areas that would be too hard to reach. The top shelves, which are barely reachable, are devoted to displaying collectibles.

Determine shelf spans by using the chart on page 168. The total length of the

shelves isn't the issue; it's the distance between supports.

Determine spacing by measuring the height of the largest books you want to store

upright and adding a couple of inches for fingertips, which makes it easier to move books in and out. While you can move adjustable shelves later, rough estimates are useful at the design stage.

In general, shelves for paperbacks need to be only $5^{1}/_{2}$ inches deep and 8 to 10 inches in height. With hardcover books, the spacing depends on the range of sizes in your collection and on how you want to sort them. If only a few books are much larger than others, design shelves for the bulk of your collection and place the oversize volumes flat or move them to a coffee table. If you have a more even mixture of sizes, you might want to design shelves for the larger ones so you can keep all sizes together.

ABOVE: Bookshelves don't have to be just uprights and crosspieces. This creative composition houses books, provides seating or display space on top, and serves as a safety rail for the stairway. The small base supports a single elevated cube and "sail" of dark wood at one end, and a larger elevated bookshelf section near the top of the stairs at the other.

LEFT: Recessing a bookcase into a wall gives it a supporting role in a living room. The white molding around the edges matches the trim around the windows.

LEFT: A rolling ladder gives easy access to bookshelves that reach all the way to a high ceiling. A ladder like this has fittings that hook over a top rail. The design allows you to conserve space by pushing in the ladder when it's not in use. The bottom of the ladder rolls on the black outrigger attachments.

Working with window seats

In living rooms, window seats serve multiple purposes. They're handy extra seating. If spacious enough, they also double as guest beds. Plus, they're great for reading, playing board games, or just gazing out into a garden or nearby street. Many people associate window seats with bay windows, which angle out on two sides, and multi-section bow windows, which curve more gently. But a straight wall often makes a better setting, provided there is space on the sides for bookcases or other features that can provide a backrest and a place to plant one's feet.

A narrow but deep alcove next to a fireplace makes a romantic reading nook. The built-in shelf provides a good place for setting down a cup of tea or a partially read book.

By the Numbers

To be comfortable and provide a great view, a window seat can't be too high, too narrow, or too low in relation to the window. There should also be a sturdy backrest for someone to sit crosswise or facing out with feet firmly on the floor. For this, the seat, including the cushion, should be no more than 18 inches from the floor. But the curl-up-with-a-book appeal of a window seat implies that the person should also be able to sit with feet up on the bench. For a person to do that comfortably, the seat needs to be deep enough—at least 22 inches and ideally more like 30 to 36 inches. There needs to be a back support that extends about 15 inches higher than the cushion. It's also helpful to have the bench short enough so the person's feet touch the far end. That's what curling up is all about. For the best view out, the bottom of the window should be within 12 inches of the top of the seat.

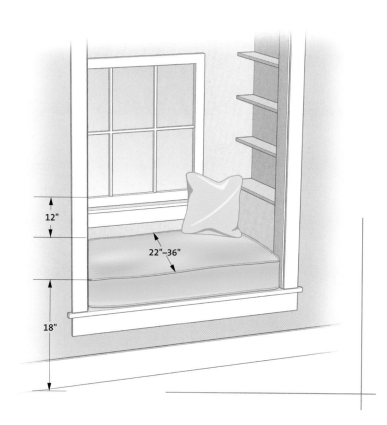

12"

22"–36"

18"

ABOVE, LEFT: **Curtains that extend in front of a window seat create an illusion that the windows and benches jut out from the building to capture as much of the sweeping view as possible.**

ABOVE, RIGHT: **In a bay or bow window, the space between the seat and the windowsill acts as a backrest. Window seats like this provide great views, but they are not as comfortable for reading or napping as smaller, more enclosed window seats.**

LEFT: **Built-in benches turn a sunny alcove off a living room into a multifunctional space. Storage and display areas are underneath and in the cantilevered drawers at each side.**

LEFT: **Setting a window seat between two bookcases not only reinforces the connection with reading, but the arrangement also provides a sturdy backrest and a foot stop for someone sitting crosswise on the cushion.**

FAR LEFT: **Where a seat runs directly across a window, protective bars add safety.**

Other ways to build in seating

Besides window seats, other kinds of built-in seating also work well in living rooms. These seats, too, should be designed so the top of the cushion or bench is no more than 18 inches from the floor. A few inches lower is even better. Seats that people will use while facing out are most comfortable if they aren't too deep. Often, 17 to 22 inches is about right. The back cushion should recline slightly so that it supports the lower back.

ABOVE: Like a window seat but without a low window, this reading nook is a great addition to a living room.

A built-in couch saves space when some of its parts are turned into storage. With a couch like this, for example, it's easy to make the back into a bookcase that's open on the hall side. Similarly, the armrest can lift up to reveal storage underneath. When closed, it's a nice flat spot for a plate of food, a glass of wine, or a good book. In case the owners want to add reading lamps, the unit includes a receptacle on the side.

This couch has storage space built into an open bookcase one end and the drawers below the seat cushions. Drawers like this are an ideal place to store bedding if the couch is likely to be pressed into service as a guest bed.

A wide, low bench in front of a built-in bookcase works as a step to the highest shelf and gives people a place to sit and read. The wide baseboard under the window visually connects the bench to the view and makes the platform seem almost like a window seat, even though it's off to the side.

Specialized uses

Built-ins can be easily customized to store everything from firewood to board games to prized collectibles. Depending on the size of the items and how many there are, you might want to estimate how much space you'll need by measuring a representative sample. With other items, such as board games, the dimensions of the largest boxes might matter most.

For firewood storage, location is everything. Keep a small amount within easy reach so you're not constantly dropping debris across the room. Store only enough for a day or two indoors, though, as firewood may contain insect pests such as termites or carpenter ants that you wouldn't want taking up permanent residence in your home.

TOP, RIGHT: **A drawer lined with foam insulation slides out on the exterior side of a wall so the homeowners can load the space with firewood. When they need to add a log to the fire, they pull out the drawer on the interior side and reach for a piece.**

ABOVE: **A built-in cabinet between the kitchen and living room includes a cubbyhole stocked with wood for an old-fashioned cookstove. The hardworking room divider also includes space for cookbooks, several drawers, and a countertop.**

LEFT: **A low bench around the perimeter of a living room steps down to provide storage for firewood. With scattered cushions, the bench offers both seating and display space.**

When built-in shelves or cabinets are used to display collectibles, design elements can play up special aspects of the objects. What better way to display a collection of art glass than on light-drenched glass shelves?

For collectibles, built-ins can help showcase items that otherwise might seem like clutter. Displaying things behind glass doors minimizes the amount of time you need to spend dusting the pieces yet still keeps them within view. For many people, one of the main goals of displaying a collection is using it to spark conversation about how they got the items or what makes each piece different. If this is your goal, build the display cabinet where guests are likely to see it.

Simple shelves supported by wooden brackets create an effective display area for several dozen wooden decoys. Collections are often most interesting when the display helps show off the contrasts and similarities among the various objects.

ADDING BUILT-INS TO A KITCHEN

Cabinet boxes don't have to be cubes. Slanting sides are used to great effect in this kitchen. The design provides extra toe space at the island and adds style to the sink cabinet.

EVEN A KITCHEN OUTFITTED WITH FULLY FUNCTIONAL, matching cabinets can benefit from the addition of a custom built-in or two. Breakfast nooks, china cabinets, spice racks, islands, desks, and shelves for cookbooks are some of the features that add personality and efficiency to a room filled with factory-made cabinets. Many of these make good projects for weekend woodworkers.

If you're an ambitious soul who wants something other than standard cabinets, you can design a whole range of built-ins—and maybe even build

them yourself if you are on a tight budget. Base and upper cabinets are, after all, just basic boxes. You can build the drawers and doors yourself, or purchase them ready-made. It's also possible to embellish existing cabinets, be it the ones in your own home, those that you buy at a bargain from a store that specializes in used building materials, or cabinets you find online. And every community has finish carpenters or small woodworking shops equipped to build custom pieces. Chapter 3 discusses all of these approaches.

What you need first, though, is an idea of the features and design elements you want.

ABOVE, LEFT: A bookcase for cookbooks makes the peninsula cabinets in this kitchen more useful.

LEFT: By opening part of a wall between the kitchen and dining room, the owners of this house gained a breakfast counter and a pass-through for food and dishes. The steps for creating an opening like this are basically the same as shown on pages 192–195.

BELOW: Building a cabinet into a wall, rather than hanging it on one, saves space and makes it seem less boxy.

STANDARD CABINET DIMENSIONS

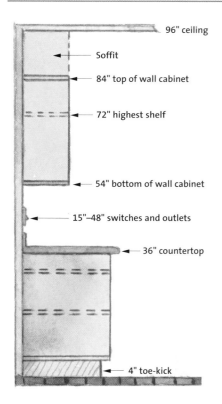

- 96" ceiling
- Soffit
- 84" top of wall cabinet
- 72" highest shelf
- 54" bottom of wall cabinet
- 15"–48" switches and outlets
- 36" countertop
- 4" toe-kick

Pull-out cutting boards and auxiliary counters are easy to add if you plan ahead, and they make a kitchen easier to use. The metal cladding on this pull-out shelf creates a safe place to set down dishes hot from a microwave.

Design principles

Over the years, people who design kitchens for a living have come up with some rules of thumb that help ensure efficient workspaces. The National Kitchen and Bath Association distills them into 40 guidelines, which you can read at www.nkba.org. You can certainly adjust some of the details, such as the height of base cabinets, to suit the height of people in your family. However, it also pays to think about what will make your kitchen most useful over the long term. Features that were once called "handicapped accessible" now tend to be called "universal design" because of a growing realization that everyone's needs change over time—sometimes even from task to task.

Set work surfaces at different heights, not just the standard 36 inches for kitchen countertops. Children and people who are seated are more comfortable at a counter about 30 inches high. Tall people appreciate one that's 45 inches high. If you're thinking of tucking a desk into the kitchen, the best height for a computer keyboard is about 25 inches for someone 5 feet tall and 30 inches for someone 6 feet tall. See page 111 for more details.

Make storage areas easier to use by equipping them with fittings that let items move toward you rather than the other way around. Instead of climbing stairs to reach high shelves, for example, outfit the shelves with pull-down hardware so they move within reach. Rather than strain to get into the back of a deep cabinet, install drawers or pullout shelves so the storage rolls forward. Temper this strategy with a financial reality check, however. Some specialized hardware is very expensive and you might not find it worth the added cost.

If you want to add a pantry but don't have space for a walk-in type, pullout pantry shelves are another option. They're a good retrofit for cabinets that are too deep to use efficiently or for awkward spaces left at the ends of cabinets.

RIGHT: A spice rack and a book-case for cookbooks are nice embellishments in this kitchen.

BELOW: A wonderful array of built-ins adds to the charm and utility of this kitchen. Besides the standard cabinets, it features built-in seating on three sides of the table. The island is equipped with a small sink and a chop-ping-block top, creating an ideal prep area. One end is outfitted for cookbook storage.

Open shelving

In some kitchens, everything stows away behind solid doors. In others, some or all of the storage space is in view on open shelves or behind glass doors, or it is tucked into a pantry. There are good reasons for each strategy. Fully enclosed storage makes life easy. You don't have to worry as much about tidiness, and the doors keep out dust. But open storage creates an airy, less formal look that better suits the style many people want in a kitchen, and it lets visitors share in cooking chores more easily. Open shelves are also perfect for pantries, which by nature are utilitarian spaces where you want to be able to see and easily retrieve what you've stored.

If you want to add storage to a kitchen already equipped with basic cabinets, built-in open shelves are a great way to go. They're inexpensive and easy to build, and they look great even if they don't match the cabinets.

ABOVE: Open shelves meet up with other horizontal surfaces in a charmingly rustic kitchen. The windowsills merge into the base of the cabinet above the cutting board, while the top trim over windows and door helps support a display shelf.

LEFT: Open shelves over a built-in bench make every inch count in this compact kitchen. Paint and fabric colors unite the two elements.

RIGHT: C-shaped shelves border three sides of this pantry closet in a design that keeps everything stored within easy view and reach. The project on pages 182–185 shows how to build custom-fitting shelves similar to these.

BELOW: Corner shelves, which are easy to build, make good use of an awkward space. The shelves are especially useful for displaying large objects that take advantage of the deep space in the middle.

ABOVE: Open shelves are perfect for pantries, but if you want to store dishes or other items for long periods, consider moving in a cabinet with doors so less dust collects on them. This arrangement incorporates a used cabinet.

LEFT: Boxed-in open shelves create two storage levels and have a more substantial look than a single shelf does. To build shelves like these, you could combine the concepts shown for building bracket shelves on pages 170–171 and basic boxes on pages 196–199.

Efficient islands

An island is a fixture of a modern kitchen, but it can play very different roles depending on how it is equipped. At its simplest, it is a work surface or staging area with storage underneath. Add a small sink and access to a compost bin, though, and an island evolves into a food-preparation area. With a cooktop, an island becomes a cooking center. With an overhang so people can pull up chairs or stools, it serves as a breakfast bar or the prime spot for sampling hors d'oeuvres during a party.

A prep island needs a sink and a cutting board, and ideally it should also incorporate storage for knives and appliances such as a blender and a food processor. You'll probably want to store heavy equipment on a movable shelf outfitted with an appliance lift so you won't have to lift the machine directly. Provide an electrical receptacle.

A downdraft fan on a cooking surface eliminates the need for an overhead hood and allows a pot rack to hang there instead. If you plan to do a lot of cooking on an island, provide space on at least one side where you can set down hot pots. The National Kitchen and Bath Association recommends a counter at least 9 inches wide on one side of a cooktop, and a counter at least 15 inches wide on the other.

BY THE NUMBERS

Between an island and another work area, such as a sink or stove, there must be a clear space of at least 42 inches, or 48 if you want two cooks to work together without getting in each other's way. Where there is just walking space alongside an island, allow at least 36 inches. An island works best if it is 2 to 4 feet wide and at least 4 feet long. If it has a sink or a cooktop, make it at least 6 feet long.

A cooking island should be designed around a cooktop and its venting needs. If you opt for an overhead hood, it rules out an overhead pot rack. But the other option, a downdraft fan, requires a duct that extends through the island, significantly reducing storage space. Besides storage for pots and pans, provide places to keep cooking oils and spices, hot pads, and utensils. If you want people to sit at an island where you also cook, consider elevating the eating area slightly to shelter diners from the spray of sizzling oil.

LEFT: A sink at one end of a prep island isn't as useful as one with ample counter space on both sides, as shown here.

BELOW: A butcher-block countertop on an island can suffice for some cutting tasks, but foods such as raw meat should still be sliced on small cutting boards that can be thoroughly washed in warm, soapy water.

ABOVE: Open shelves facing the dining room side of an island keep dishes in clear view. If you're worried about crumbs spilling over from the island, recess the shelves slightly.

RIGHT: An island with seating on both sides has space in the middle for a narrow wine rack, which doubles as support for the countertop.

Breakfast nooks

Breakfast nooks are among the most popular built-ins. They are friendly and space efficient and in most cases quite easy to build. Some nooks incorporate a built-in table, while others have only the seating built in. The benches-plus-table type are the most space efficient, as they require only a single leg in front if the back of the table is attached to the wall. But nooks with movable tables provide the most flexibility, and the table can be moved out of the way when it's time to mop the floor. Either style eliminates the need for leaving a couple of feet free behind chairs so there's room for people to pull them out while getting up or down.

ABOVE, LEFT: **When built-in benches run along both sides of a corner, even a tiny eat-in kitchen becomes big enough for a gang of kids to dine comfortably with two adults in chairs.**

ABOVE, RIGHT: **Curved brackets support the seats and single table leg in this nook, giving it a slightly Victorian look. Benches supported only by end brackets are more comfortable than those with full cabinets underneath, because the open space allows diners to tuck their feet back.**

Angled support braces hold up both the seats and the tabletop in this diminutive breakfast nook, allowing it to fit into an especially compact space. Because the table has no legs, it's easy for diners to scoot in and out. Baseboard heaters along the walls keep the space toasty.

The simplest type of nook consists of a
built-in bench plus a movable table and
chairs. The steps required to build a bench
like this are shown on pages 176–179.

Make it comfortable

In a restaurant, people often gravitate toward booths on the edges rather than tables in the center. The booths are more comfortable, and they make it easier to hear what a person on the other side of the table is saying. Plus, if a window is on one wall, there are the added benefits of a view and natural light, at least for breakfast and lunch. Similar features make home dining nooks attractive.

Round or oval tables always seem able to accommodate one more diner. Nooks with curved seating offer the same benefit. Comfort features of this design include the wide overhang on the bench and cushions that support the lower back.

By the Numbers

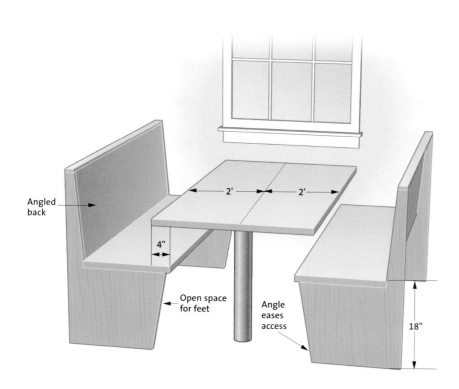

Angled back

2'   2'

4"

Open space for feet

Angle eases access

18"

Tables 30 inches high and 32 to 36 inches wide work well when there is seating on only two sides. Angled backrests are more comfortable than ones that rise straight up, because of their added support for the lower back. The table should overlap the seats by about 4 inches on each side. Allow about 2 feet of table length per adult. For wider spaces, provide a U-shaped bench. A base that angles back at the bottom or is open underneath also adds comfort because it allows people to tuck their feet back. Seats should be 18 to 20 inches wide and about 18 inches high, including the cushions.

Angled base cabinets, angled back-rests, and thick cushions all add to the comfort of this dining nook. The U-shaped bench and a couple of chairs provide room for eight adults or maybe a dozen kids.

Padded seats add comfort to a dining nook and make it resemble a booth at a restaurant.

IN THE BATHROOM

BATHROOMS OF ALL SIZES ARE PERFECT FOR BUILT-INS, which provide space for basics such as towels, toiletries, and cleaning supplies. Bathroom storage usually starts with a cabinet known as a vanity, except when there is a pedestal sink. In that case, a wall-mounted shelf or perhaps a multi-shelf setup often suffices. After that, built-in possibilities vary according to how much space there is. Popular additions include larger storage cabinets, a bench, and a makeup counter.

RIGHT: Symmetry adds to the elegance of this luxurious bathroom. Twin vanities and open cabinets for towels and toiletries frame the oval tub at the end of the room. The tall cabinets divide the space into zones for bathing and dressing.

BELOW: A two-tier countertop keeps the sink within reach of children yet allows adults to keep decorative items at a slightly higher level. Tall cabinets to the left provide abundant space for towels.

In bathrooms with pedestal sinks, storage is often confined to a few wall shelves. Flanking the sink with base cabinets provides a lot more space.

In bathrooms with a little extra room, a built-in bench is a welcome addition. It beats fumbling on one leg while you're trying to pull a sock onto the other foot. There's nice variety in this room. Even though the vanity and a pair of tall cabinets are made of matching wood, the bathroom still has a relaxed, "unfitted" feel because the vanity sits on legs while the tall cabinets are on bases.

Vanities

Bathroom cabinets vary more than kitchen cabinets, which are usually about 36 inches high and 24 inches deep, including the countertop and base. The National Kitchen and Bath Association recommends vanity heights of 32 to 43 inches, depending on the users' needs. Mostly that means tall people like vanities at the higher end of that range, while shorter people prefer them lower. But whatever your height, if you plan to sit down to put on makeup or shave, you'll find a low counter more convenient. You might even want counters at more than one height.

Cabinet depths also vary. The standard is 21 inches deep, but in small bathrooms, consider cabinets that are 16 or 18 inches. If you need something even shallower, switch to a semi-recessed sink, which projects beyond the countertop. Some sit on cabinets only about 9 inches deep—not great for storage but better than nothing.

Cabinet widths typically vary in 3-inch increments, just like kitchen cabinets. They range from 18 to 60 inches wide. For custom sizes or designs, hire a local cabinetmaker or consider building your own. Tackling a single vanity isn't as daunting as building cabinets for an entire kitchen. Manufactured cabinets come with various combinations of drawers and shelves. Drawers are generally more useful than shelves.

BATHROOM FIXTURE CLEARANCES

Double sink

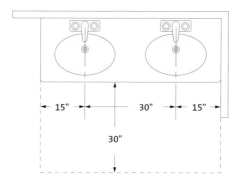

Toilet

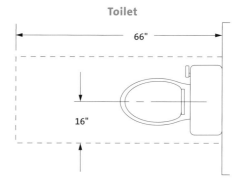

Bathtub

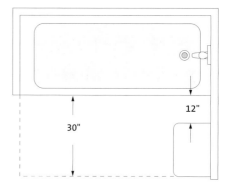

Hidden Step

There's no way to install a bathroom sink so it's at the perfect height for everyone, so a built-in stepstool makes a lot of sense. This custom design, by Michael Meyer Fine Woodworking, has casters mounted on springs that hold the box off the floor by about $1/4$ inch. The box easily rolls out from the cabinet on these casters. Then, when someone steps on the box, the casters retract and the box drops to the floor. It's stable and solid on the floor until the person steps off, at which point the casters spring back and raise the box so it can be rolled back into its garage.

LEFT: Vanities with abundant built-in storage and toe-kick spaces can be designed to resemble furniture-style vanities. This example has mock feet at the corners, and it stops a short distance from the wall. If you opt for a design like this, leave enough of a gap so that you can reach into the corner to clean.

BELOW: On a long counter with two sinks, it's possible to sacrifice some countertop space to gain more storage. The lift-up door at the bottom of the center cabinet hides a hair dryer or other items and keeps them from cluttering the counter.

Floating vanities

Besides vanities that rest on furniture legs or bases, there are models designed to hang on a wall. Often called floating vanities, they look lighter and leave more of the floor open. These are the same features that often prompt people to opt for pedestal sinks. But floating vanities work better in many bathrooms. They provide significant storage and have roomier countertops, and they can be custom-designed to fit the available space. Pedestal sinks come from factories, so sizes are set.

LEFT: **A wall-hung vanity can provide almost as much countertop space and drawer storage as a unit on a base, sacrificing only the lowest drawers.**

BOTTOM, LEFT: **Though relatively large, this bathroom would seem uncomfortably cramped if the vanity extended to the floor. Hanging it from the wall creates the visual space needed for the fireplace.**

BOTTOM, RIGHT: **In a tiny space, a wall-hung vanity still manages to accommodate a relatively spacious counter, two sinks, and storage in the baskets underneath.**

A partial wall covered with tile curls around one end of a wall-hung vanity. The tile detail then continues its run as the curb for the shower.

Vanities in powder rooms

If you want a sleek little vanity that prances in high style but offers little in the way of storage, a powder room is a good place to indulge. The stylish look may be very important to you given that this is the bathroom you'll show to your guests. Sacrificing storage space may be no big deal, as powder rooms don't generally need much anyway. They certainly don't need a place to put stacks of bath towels, since powder rooms lack showers. Powder rooms also tend to be easier to keep clean than other bathrooms because they aren't subjected to shower steam or left littered with dirty clothes. This matters as you're planning a powder room vanity because it frees you to consider materials, such as a glass countertop, that might require too frequent cleaning in a different bathroom. Of course, there's no rule against putting a standard vanity cabinet with a few drawers or shelves in a powder room. It's just not as much fun.

This vanity incorporates as much storage as many people have in family bathrooms, but it sits in a powder room. That's clear from two details: the tiny sink, suitable only for washing hands, and the decorations. Historical photographs don't fare well near steamy showers.

Beautiful wood paneling and doors pair up with a polished granite counter and a brushed metal sink in this powder room. Even though storage needs aren't great in powder rooms, you may still want to design the vanity to hold spare toilet tissue. Keeping an extra roll where guests can find it prevents embarrassing moments.

DESIGN TIP

If a powder room is very small, increase its usable space by installing a sliding door or one that swings out. Consider adding a handrail beside the toilet for guests who need the extra support. Store hand towels, spare toilet paper, and paper cups where guests can find what they need without having to ask. If you want the powder room to stay ready for guest use, keep toothbrushes and other items used only by family members in another bathroom, or at least store them in drawers or behind closed doors.

An artful composition of stacked stone creates a striking vanity for a powder room. Stone veneer, which is about as easy to install as tile, forms the front and wall surround, while a thick slab of stone with a rough, chipped edge supports the mosaic vessel sink.

Other bathroom built-ins

Besides vanities, other built-ins enhance bathrooms. A makeup counter is popular, but to work well it needs to be about 28 inches high, considerably lower than the standard 36 inches of kitchen countertops. The lower height allows someone to put on makeup, shave, and attend to their grooming while sitting in a chair.

If you have a large bathroom, you might consider adding an island, which provides storage space as well as a countertop where you can set out clean clothes. Other built-in luxuries include fireplaces and additional storage cabinets.

In a small bathroom, shelving set into a wall or a series of bracket shelves attached to the surface can do wonders. You might also consider adding a storage unit that straddles the toilet tank and provides shelving above. But don't build in storage there. The unit should be easy to move to allow a plumbing repair.

TOP, LEFT: **This countertop steps down as it transitions from the vanity to the makeup desk, creating surfaces you can use comfortably while standing or sitting. Makeup counters equipped with standard chairs should be about the same height as a dining room table.**

LEFT: **A gas fireplace warms a bathroom and looks far classier than a heat lamp or a toe-kick vent.**

In a small bathroom, replacing a little-used tub with a shower may create enough space for built-in storage and a shower.

ABOVE: The owners of this home designed and built the cabinets and intersecting bench in a corner of this sunny bathroom. Towels tuck into the corner, making clever use of a space that's usually awkward to reach.

LEFT: A cute little makeup desk with two tiny drawers fits between a pair of tall cabinets. If you didn't need the drawers, you could build a similar desk by installing an alcove shelf, as shown on pages 174–175.

ABOVE, LEFT: An island in a bathroom helps separate bathing and dressing areas and provides storage for towels or other bulky items. The countertop is a great place to set out fresh clothing.

RIGHT: Cabinets under the eaves add elegance and storage to a small bathroom. The half wall adds privacy.

Built-in medicine cabinets can depart from the traditional look of a mirrored door that opens to shelves behind. This design marries the door to ribbon-like floating shelves.

Cabinets

Small bathrooms especially benefit from built-in medicine cabinets and shelves that are recessed into a wall. Such features add storage without infringing on floor space.

One less-than-obvious place for recessed shelves is behind the bathroom door. Just make sure the wall there is not an exterior one, where you wouldn't want to compromise the insulation. By extending the shelves into the stud space and taking advantage of the gap left between the wall and the door for trim, these shelves can usually be 6 to 8 inches deep, not generous but enough for toiletries or that longtime bathroom necessity, good books. On pages 192–195, you'll find instructions for opening a wall so that you can install a medicine cabinet or shelf unit into it.

Although it's common to mount a built-in medicine cabinet behind a sink, it's not possible to recess a cabinet there if pipes are hidden in the wall. This bathroom has a large mirror on the wall behind the two sinks. A built-in medicine cabinet tucks nicely into a sidewall.

ABOVE: A short and judiciously placed wall creates an alcove for a pedestal tub and provides a base for inset shelves next to the sink.

FAR LEFT: A built-in bookcase is a welcome addition to a bathroom, unless you're the person waiting outside for the door to open.

LEFT: Projecting into the room no more than a standard mirror would, a recessed medicine cabinet provides two essentials: a mirror on the door and much-needed storage above a pedestal sink.

ABOVE: A small cabinet attached to the wall or partially recessed into it provides handy storage. A glass door is especially useful in a guest bathroom that's used infrequently. The door keeps out dust yet allows guests to find what they need on their own.

RIGHT: Extending the base of a boxed-in tub provides storage for towels and creates a more generous ledge around the tub.

Places for towels

With towels, some of the usual issues involved in bathroom storage are just wiped away. There's nothing private or embarrassing about towels, and they look attractive. So there is no need to squirrel them away behind closed doors or in drawers. They're not unsafe, either, so, unlike medicine, for example, they can be left in easy reach of even young children.

There are two important issues about storing towels, however: their bulk and the need to have a dry towel within reach when you emerge from a shower or bath. Cleverly designed built-ins allow you to deal with both issues at once.

There's no need to track drips across a floor when towels are kept on shelves at the end of the tub. Because of the danger of slipping if you have to stretch to reach, high shelves work best only for display.

FAR LEFT: A knee wall, which encloses space on an upper floor where the roof slants down, houses inset shelves deep enough to store even bulky bath towels. The shelves are within easy reach of the shower.
LEFT: Walls framing a dormer window may also accommodate built-in shelves.

IN THE BEDROOM

ADDING BUILT-INS TO A BEDROOM can solve more than storage problems. Bookcases, cabinets, window seats and other solutions create a cozier room. These features can fit into or along walls, or they can function as walls. You can use them to divide a large room into a sleeping area and one that you use for another purpose, such as a home office or a hobby room. Built-ins that function as room dividers can incorporate storage, wiring for lights, and even plumbing.

LEFT: Tucked into the alcove created by a dormer window, a window seat is spacious enough to double as a guest bed—or two, since a trundle bed fits into the space below. Small doors on both sides provide access to storage space behind the knee walls.

OPPOSITE, TOP: Closets, a bureau, and a makeup vanity are some of the improvements that can be built into a bedroom. One advantage of installing built-ins rather than using furniture for these purposes is that built-ins don't need to be moved periodically for cleaning.

OPPOSITE, BOTTOM: Where built-in closets flank a bedroom window, the space in between makes an ideal location for a built-in window seat.

DESIGN TIP

When a bedroom needs to double as a place to sleep and an office, use built-ins to create separate areas or mini-rooms for each activity. If you share the room, make the built-ins high enough so you can work without shining light into your partner's eyes. Determining the height is a two-person job: One lies flat on the bed, the other measures. See pages 100–101 for more design tips.

Headboards

A built-in headboard can transform a bedroom. This is true whether the room is large or small, but the room's size often influences the type of headboard and its purpose. In spacious bedrooms, a high headboard can serve as a room divider. This might be especially useful in a home where one person wants to sleep in while another needs to be up early to get dressed for work. A headboard room divider could also be used to create an office space in a large bedroom. In a small bedroom, a built-in headboard is more likely to serve as a storage area for books or other items.

Whatever the purpose, there are some important features to keep in mind.

• **PROVIDE A BACKREST** directly behind the pillows that's comfortable to lean against and tall enough so you don't hit your back or head on whatever is above. This part of a headboard doubles as a backrest if you sit up in bed to read, watch TV, or type on a laptop.

• **INCLUDE READING LIGHTS** at the right height. The bottom of the shade should be about 20 inches above the pillow. Any lower and there won't be enough light on pages; any higher and the bulb will shine in your eyes.

• **INCORPORATE NIGHTSTANDS** on both sides of the bed (or on one side of a twin bed). Provide flat surfaces big enough for a book, a glass of water, and an alarm clock.

If you want the comfort of a padded headboard but need storage, this arrangement is one solution. The headboard isn't built in, but the bookcases are. Each has a cavity at the bottom so a nightstand table can be tucked in when you need more room next to the bed, such as when it's time to make the bed.

A headboard-bookcase combination provides all the essentials: an obstruction-free backrest, a reading light at the right height, a nightstand, and even a niche for family pictures.

If a tall headboard isn't a feature you covet, a setup like this provides abundant storage, good light for reading in bed, and a serene scene. Countertops on either side provide additional space for setting drinks or books.

Light switches are conveniently close to the head of the bed on the back portion of this multilayer headboard. The inner section rises at a slight angle, the better to support the lower back when someone sits up to read or watch TV. The drawer units double as nightstands. The wood in the headboard unit matches that of the bookcase and the bed, underscoring the built-in look.

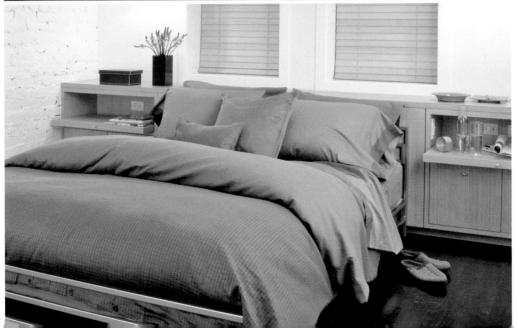

Attached to the wall as if they were upper cabinets in a kitchen, two nightstand cabinets flank a center section that works as a backrest. The nightstands are wired in so people can control the lights without getting out of bed.

Built-in beds

Where space is tight or you need a bed to function as a couch or window seat part of the time, a built-in bed with storage often makes sense. If you build a bed along a wall, expect to trade away a little convenience because it will be harder to change sheets. If you add storage underneath, the bed may be slightly higher than usual and the storage may be so low that you'll need to crouch to use it. But in return, you'll gain multiple uses in your space.

Shop for the mattress before you build the bed, so you're sure the sizes will work well together. If your space doesn't suit a standard mattress size, consider purchasing a piece of high-density foam cut to fit. Crib mattresses are big enough for youth beds that will see most kids through primary grades.

Standard Mattress Sizes

Be sure to actually measure the mattress before you buy. Some manufacturers go by sizes that differ from these customary dimensions by an inch or more.

Mattress Type	Width × Length, in Inches
Crib	28 × 52
Twin ("single")	39 × 75
Extra-long twin	39 × 80
Double ("full")	54 × 75
Queen	60 × 80
King	76 × 80
California king	72 × 84

When beds incorporate storage, it's usually in drawers under the bed. But shelves set into a wall beside the bed are also useful.

Tucked into a short but relatively wide space, this would be a magical bed for a visiting grandchild. During the day, a creative youngster would probably turn it into a prop for all sorts of fantasy adventures.

Built like the window seat project on pages 176–179, this couch doubles as a guest bed. Bedding could be stored in a lift-up seat under the cushion. The curtains provide privacy when a guest is staying but allow the space to be opened up at other times.

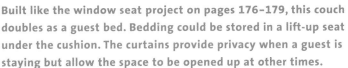

TOP, RIGHT: This built-in headboard creates a sense of enclosure, especially when the doors are pulled close to the bed, and it houses reading and mood lights over the pillows.

ABOVE: In the same space that a stand-alone bed would require, this built-in manages to accommodate not only a mattress but also two sets of recessed shelves, two small closets, and two large drawers. The brackets and cornice make the space seem like a semiprivate nook.

Built-in beds with storage underneath are often called captain's beds, presumably because they mimic features of the boss's quarters on a ship. A vaulted ceiling enhances this theme, as does the nautical lamp.

Guest beds

If you can devote a spare room to being a guest bedroom, a standard bed works fine. However, a built-in may be a better choice if the guest room also has to function as something else, such as an office or a crafts room. Built-in beds are more adaptable to being used as couches or benches, and you can easily design them to provide storage space as well. There are several styles.

Murphy beds, which swing upright against a wall when not in use, are one popular option. They operate on hardware that uses pistons or springs. When a bed is in the up position, people in the room may think they're seeing only wood paneling.

Loft beds have a lot of storage underneath—so much, in fact, that you may need to use a ladder to climb up to the mattress.

Window seat beds are another option. They differ from ordinary window seats only in size. The cushion needs to be big enough for a person to stretch out. If the cushion is about 3 feet wide and a little more than 6 feet long, you can use twin fitted sheets tucked in at the sides and end. A piece of dense foam makes a good mattress.

TOP: **Most of the time, what appears to be a comfortable couch sits slightly recessed into a paneled alcove with a mirror and two metal decorations.**

RIGHT: **When guests arrive, the homeowners move the cushions to the side and pull on the metal decorations. The panel folds down to reveal a mattress. The metal decorations pivot out and become legs. The owners move the couch cushions back into place to create a padded headboard. For a setup like this, you'd need the type of Murphy bed mechanism that operates on pistons attached to the sides of the alcove, not a spring type that attaches to the floor.**

If you have a window seat in a guest bed-room, adding curtains creates a secluded space for a child who might need to go to bed earlier than her parents.

A pull-down bed allows a small room, such as one over a garage or in an attic, to double as a crafts room, office, or play room when the bed is not needed.

Loft beds

A loft bed, as the name implies, is usually too high to reach without a ladder or step-stool. Because the access is awkward, this kind of bed is often reserved for occasional use, either by a guest or by a host family's child who has given up his or her bedroom for a guest's use.

If a child will use a loft bed, even if just as a play space, add rails, as you'd do with a top bunk bed. To avoid creating spaces where a child's head might get caught, make sure that gaps between rails and between a rail and the mattress are less than $3\frac{1}{2}$ inches wide. The U.S. Consumer Product Safety Commission says that children younger than six shouldn't be allowed to sleep on high beds.

A loft bed fits into one end of a cathedral ceiling. The ladder design incorporates several safety features. Uprights extend past the top step to provide a handhold for someone climbing onto or off of the ladder. Rungs are notched into the uprights, not merely nailed or screwed on. And openings are more than 9 inches tall so they won't trap a child's head.

RIGHT: An oversize day-bed, with its own built-in step, is a great place for an adult to read or nap. Given the windows all around, kids are likely to see it as a tree house and turn it into a fort.

BELOW: Even if a loft bed is only used for play, it has decorative value. If children will use a bed like this to sleep in, provide a ladder that can't be knocked loose, install a rail, and avoid placing hooks or handles where kids might get caught or tangled in hanging belts or clothing when climbing up or down.

RIGHT: A rolling ladder, like the ones often found in libraries, provides a safe route up to this loft bed and storage area. This type of ladder can be pushed upright to save space, as seen here. The ladder can be pulled out at a safe angle when in use.

Defining spaces

By positioning a built-in to serve as a full or partial wall, you may be able to create an office, dressing room, sewing nook, or other separate space from what is now just a bedroom. This type of built-in can also solve other problems, such as a lack of storage space and an awkward room arrangement that puts the bed where it gets too much light for you to sleep in on weekends. To design a built-in like this:

- MEASURE THE ROOM, using the procedure discussed on pages 166–167.
- MAKE A SCALE DRAWING and cut out scaled pieces that represent your bed, bureaus, or other furniture, as well as potential room dividers in several sizes.
- EXPERIMENT WITH ROOM ARRANGEMENTS until you find one you like. Be sure to allow enough space to get from one area to another. In most cases, that means leaving walkways at least 2 feet wide, though 3 feet is even better; 18 inches might do in a pinch, such as along one side of a bed where you just need room to get in and out and change sheets. Also leave enough space to pull out drawers and still stand in front of them. Doors need space to swing, unless you switch to more space-saving types, such as sliding or bifold doors.

A tall built-in cabinet packs in a variety of storage options and improves the *feng shui* aspects of this room, because it shelters the bed and prevents it from directly facing the door.

LEFT: A room-dividing cabinet allowed a bed to be turned around so that it faces windows but isn't right underneath them. One side of the cabinet serves as a headboard, and a dresser is on the other. Bookshelves fit into the ends of the cabinet.

A low built-in cabinet anchors a bed that sits in the center of a room, keeping it from seeming marooned. Wiring built into the nightstand alcoves controls reading lights, clock radios, laptops, or other gear.

FAR LEFT: A built-in headboard and bed-surround create a more intimate space in a large bedroom with a high ceiling. The back of the headboard, which faces the door, holds storage cabinets.

LEFT: The other side includes a panel that tilts out to create a backrest. The panel pushes back into an upright position at bedtime. Pillars rest on bases that double as nightstands and storage cabinets.

Low cubbies and cabinets work wonderfully in children's rooms. Even young kids can get their toys in and out, and older ones can use the top surface as a workbench.

WHAT IS KID-SIZE?

At age 2, when children first begin to use built-ins, their average height is about 3 feet. Over the next 10 years, they usually sprout up about 2 feet. If you are designing built-ins that will see kids through all these years, it often makes sense to go with the heights shown here. They are based on what works best for a child 45 inches tall, typically around age 5 or 6.

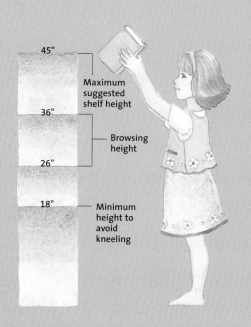

45"

Maximum suggested shelf height

36"

Browsing height

26"

18"

Minimum height to avoid kneeling

Freeing up space in children's rooms

Because children use their bedrooms for playing as well as sleeping, open areas on the floor are often at a premium. Built-ins help free up more space. If you build shelves or drawers into the bed, for example, you might be able to do without a bureau, so you gain that space to use for something else. Or build a loft, which doubles the floor space. Put a bed on top of the loft or underneath it, leaving the other area free for a desk, storage, or play space. You can also construct a loft bed over a ground-level bed aligned at a right angle. This has the double-deck function of bunk beds but makes the bottom bed feel less confining. Provide at least 30 inches of headroom above a bed and an overhead surface, whether that's the ceiling or the underside of a loft's floor.

Built-in storage in children's rooms can also serve more than one purpose. A low bench by a window, for example, might store toys underneath and provide seating on top. It can also double as a play cookstove or store counter.

A window seat in a child's room serves all the purposes of a window seat elsewhere, plus it's likely to be used for play. Kids tend to be more adaptable than adults, so they're likely to use a window seat even if its height or width isn't ideal.

Children don't need as much closet space for hanging clothes as adults typically do, so a cabinet with a short hanging area and drawers below may suffice for both a closet and a bureau. In this room, a built-in shelf meets up with the molding that divides sections of a built-in cabinet, adding a stylish detail.

LEFT: Designed like a room within a room, a built-in closet ends shy of the ceiling so there's space above for a collection of stuffed animals. The window on the closet wall brings in natural light. A young child doesn't need a big closet, so the structure could serve as a playhouse for a few years and then be converted into a closet for the teenage years.

BELOW: A built-in desk fits between the closet and a bedroom wall.

Outfitting closets

There are two basic types of bedroom closets: reach-ins and walk-ins. Both benefit from built-in enhancements.

Reach-in closets fit into a wall and have doors that open into the bedroom. The amount of hanging space you need usually drives the design of any built-in components, such as shelves or drawers. To free up space for the built-ins, consider installing a high rod and a low one where you now hang just a single row of clothes. Or group garments, such as shirts and jackets, that don't hang as low as dresses and robes do. Install the drawers or shelves below the short items.

Walk-in closets occupy rooms or alcoves, so they usually have more space for built-ins. If the closet is at least 6½ feet wide, you can hang clothes on both sides and add drawers and shelves along the back wall. Or group short items and install the built-ins underneath. If the closet is narrower than 6½ feet, consider hanging clothes on only one side and installing shallow built-ins on the other.

Only large closets have room for islands. Besides providing extra drawers or shelves, islands give you a place to set out hats, gloves, or the next day's clothing.

Stuff Within Reach

Design closet built-ins so you can place regularly used items between waist height and eye level, if possible. Put out-of-season clothes or other items you use less frequently on upper shelves or on lower shelves or drawers. Heights are based on a 69-inch-tall man and a 65-inch-tall woman.

In a children's closet, it's inevitable that some sections will be too high for kids to reach. The trade-off here devotes maximum space to drawers, which are easy for kids to use.

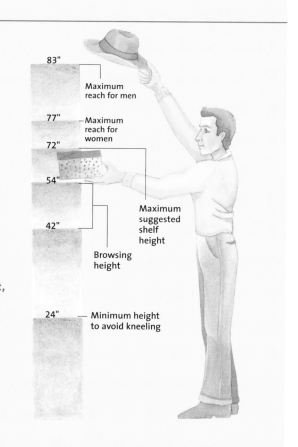

83" Maximum reach for men

77" Maximum reach for women

72"

54" Maximum suggested shelf height

42" Browsing height

24" Minimum height to avoid kneeling

LEFT: Built-in closet elements can expand the available storage space and still preserve important features in a room, such as natural light from a high window. This setup includes built-in bureaus, upper cabinets, and short hanging areas for pants and skirts.

BOTTOM, LEFT & RIGHT: Companies that specialize in closet makeovers supply shelves, drawers, and fittings for customizing closets of all sizes. You can buy just the components or purchase them with design and installation included.

Other bedroom built-ins

Closets need to be at least 24 inches deep or the doors won't clear clothes on hangers. But shelves and drawers that open directly into the room aren't locked into this minimum, so you can often fit cabinets into a bedroom even when there isn't space for an extra closet. If you need extra hanging space but want to work it into a wall system less than 24 inches deep, install rods that extend outward. Attach them either with a bracket at the back or a mechanism that slides along a shelf above.

TOP, RIGHT: A rod that extends outward allows you to hang clothing in a space less than 24 inches deep.

RIGHT: Low cabinets provide as much storage as half a dozen bureaus but leave this room uncluttered and open. The dark color of the wall and drawers provides a nice contrast to the light ceilings in this sun-drenched room.

An art collection is shown to its best advantage in a room that features crisp white walls and an equally clean built-in wall system. Recessing the TV makes it less dominant. Storing electronic gear in open cubbies keeps the controls accessible and provides air circulation so it doesn't overheat.

ABOVE: The components may be ordinary, but their placement is clever. The recessed TV cabinet, fireplace, and round window are balanced asymmetrically. The hearth unites the elements and provides a narrow display space at one end and a wider window seat at the other.

A narrow window seat breaks up a wall of built-in drawers and provides a handy place to sit while you pull on socks or tie shoelaces.

CREATING EFFICIENT HOME OFFICES

WELL-THOUGHT-OUT BUILT-INS make a home office a joy to use. It's easier to focus on tasks and complete them when files, reference materials, a computer, and whatever other tools you need are in one place and at the right height. There is no one-size-fits-all plan for a home office. A lot depends on whether you are creating a full-time office in a dedicated room or setting up a small workspace that you will use just a few hours a week.

As with built-ins in other rooms, you can build what you want from scratch, assemble it from cabinets or cabinet components, or combine built-ins with stand-alone furniture. For example, you might decide to buy a desk and a small file cabinet but build in a wall unit with open bookshelves on top and deeper cabinets with drawers and shelves below. Or you could build in the desk by extending a countertop between base cabinets that you place far enough apart to make an opening for a chair.

If the office will be used mostly to pay bills, organize mail, and keep track of household paperwork, you might want to build cubbies for each person's mail and set up a file folder or even an entire drawer for other paperwork related to that person. File folders make great places to store classroom artwork until you can sort through it and decide what's worth keeping.

DESIGN TIP

If you use standard cabinets as components, omit the usual toe-kick base so that chairs with casters on their feet can slide in and out.

Though tiny, a message center tucked into one corner of a kitchen functions as head-quarters for a busy household. The family calendar, phone book, cookbooks, laptop, and other essentials are all kept here.

ABOVE, LEFT: Built-in upper cabinets plus a small writing desk with drawers equal a home office for paying bills and taking care of correspondence. With its handsome glass doors, this setup looks sufficiently non-business that you could fit it into any room, from a bedroom to the living room or dining room.

ABOVE, RIGHT: A simple office consists of basic built-in shelves and a countertop that's attached to the wall at the back and supported by legs at the front. Though lacking in frills, this setup contains all the essentials: phone, printer, computer, work surface at an appropriate height, adjustable chairs, nearby places for pencils and the like, and storage for discs and a few books.

LEFT: If you work at home in a busy household, you may need to close yourself off from some of the hubbub without losing the ability to monitor what's going on. Sliding French doors are a good solution.

Computer ergonomics

Most home offices are centered around a computer. Even if you don't work full time from your house, if you think you may spend more than a few hours a day in front of the screen and keyboard, design your built-in around a work surface that is the right height.

Old-fashioned office desks are usually 29 or 30 inches high. That's fine if you are 6 feet or taller, but to avoid wrist and back strain, you need to work at a surface that is level with your elbows when your forearms and thighs are parallel to the floor and your feet are on the floor (see chart on opposite page).

• ADJUSTABLE FEATURES allow people of different heights to use a home office comfortably. A keyboard tray, which pulls out from underneath a desktop, is one way to create a dual-height surface. Be sure the tray is big enough so the mouse fits on it to avoid wrist strain. Adjustable chairs help bring arms to the right position in relationship to the keyboard and mouse, but they can't adjust for the correct foot position at the same time. That's why it's so important to have the desk at the right height.

• GLARE is another issue to consider. Although it's appealing to think about sitting by a window as you type at your computer, bright sunlight behind the screen is blinding. Unless the window faces north or is shaded by an awning or substantial tree, consider orienting the desk so you face a wall and have the window on your side.

When a desk extends along one wall, it's usually necessary to add task lighting for the work area, as a person working at the desk would block light from the overhead fixture and cause shadows. At this desk, the computer tower is under the work area—not ideal from an ergonomics perspective. Putting it at one end of the desk or within a cabinet would be better because it would allow users to stretch out their legs.

Before computers, desks were high enough to fit two file drawers underneath. Today, because of the lower heights needed for computer work, it's more common to have a single file drawer and one or two shallower drawers.

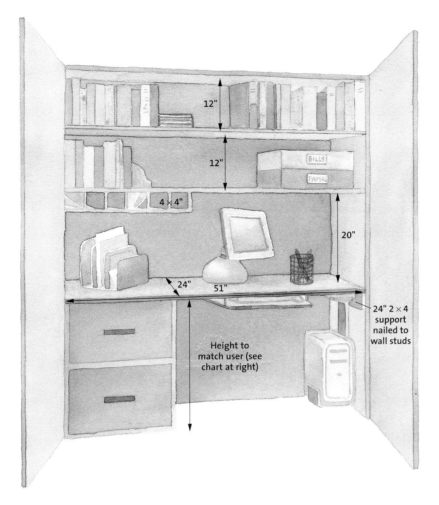

Work Surface Height

PERSON'S HEIGHT	DESK HEIGHT
5'0"–5'3"	25"–26"
5'4"–5'6"	26"–27"
5'7"–6'0"	27"–30"
6'1"–6'5"	30"–32"

This sketch shows dimensions that result in a comfortable workspace, using a desk built into a closet as an example. See more ideas for fitting offices into closets on page 117.

Nestled into a wide landing at the top of a stairway, this home office is set up for the whole family to use. Keyboard trays allow younger children to work at a lower height than parents or teenagers, who can move the keyboards and mice up to the desktop. The built-in shelves and counter hold reference books, a globe and CDs. A computer and printer fit inside in the center cabinet.

The perfect desk

As you fine-tune the details you want in a desk, think about how you work and what features would make your tasks easier. If you need a lot of flat surfaces so you can spread out projects, for example, you might want to make your desk a peninsula or an island so that you can also have a countertop behind your chair, parallel to your desk. By swiveling around, you could then reach the counter or the desk without getting up. Or, if you need the extra space only occasionally, you might want to install pullout counters, like breadboards in a kitchen.

Almost everyone needs nearby drawers or shelves for small items, such as pencils, paperclips, and paper. Small cubbies, similar to those in rolltop desks, help keep desk clutter to a minimum.

ABOVE, LEFT: Although desks that face into a wall are most common, there's no reason one can't extend out at a right angle to book-shelves.

ABOVE, RIGHT: If you need space to set out papers for large projects, consider a U-shaped desk. By swiveling your chair around, you could reach three counter sections without getting up.

LEFT: An L-shaped desk can have storage under one leg of the L and an open area under the other where you can stretch out your legs. The open area also lets you scoot the chair in when you're not using the office. That's a considera-tion for this office just inside a back door, where there might have been a mudroom. The cubbies give the family a place to stash the stray belongings that tend to col-lect next to a back door. The cur-tains block glare yet allow natural light to stream in above.

Home offices for serious work

If you plan to do paying work from home, you'll need an office where you can toil in comfort for long periods. You can't compromise on essentials such as ergonomics, natural light, and storage.

Before you invest in outfitting a space with built-ins, consider whether the room is the best location for a home office. If clients, customers, or employees will be coming to your house, you might want to put the office in a room with a separate entrance or at least in one that has an entry route that won't take visitors past parts of your home that you want to keep private.

If you have young children at home, you may need the office to be within earshot of their activities. Or you might want to be sufficiently separated from them so you can concentrate on work. It all depends on your situation.

Assess storage needs by sorting through your papers, books, and any tools or supplies you need for your work. Decide what you really need to keep. Then you'll have a good idea of how much space to allot to bookcases, cabinets with deeper shelves, file drawers, other drawers, and work surfaces.

Deep cubbies keep architectural drawings from wrinkling. They also support a high counter that a person can use while standing or while sitting on a bar stool, which is when the built-in foot rail comes in handy.

Sitting face to face, with computer screens between them, two people can work comfortably in this home office. Its features include abundant built-in storage space, both open and behind doors, and lots of natural light. Neither desk faces a wall, and both people have a window on the side where they can look out.

Provide natural light, which perks up your spirits and allows you to cut back on how much electricity you need. It's especially important in a full-time home office, which tends to be used during the daytime more than other types of home offices. High windows or ones to the side of your desk work best because they minimize glare.

Orient your desk so there's something pleasant to look at when you talk on the phone. Spending all day at home at a desk that faces a wall isn't much better than working against a wall in an office building. A home office with a desk that juts out into the room feels less claustrophobic.

A setup like this would work well as an all-day office in a quiet house or in one with a room dedicated to work. The owner can twirl around to look outside during long phone calls or scoot the other way to the spacious, curved desktop for tasks that don't require typing.

A copier fits into a custom drawer under stairs leading to a home office.

If clients will visit a home office regularly, outfit it to create a businesslike look. It may seem like a cliché, but built-ins made of dark wood convey authority and seriousness, while padded chairs tell visitors you want them to be comfortable.

A modest home office, complete with its own built-in storage space, fits under a stairway. This solution works especially well in houses with high ceilings and with stairs that turn. These features create more space under the stairs.

Tucking offices into little-used spaces

Most houses weren't built with offices in mind, but they often have small spaces that can be made to work. Luckily, the challenge is getting easier all the time because computer equipment is becoming smaller and less tethered to complicated wiring. Closets and spaces under stairways are two good options.

Closets are about 2 feet deep if they are the reach-in type and even deeper if they are walk-ins. That means an empty closet should always have room for at least a small office, since a good depth for a desk is 2 feet. Add shelves above and drawers below, buy a good chair, deal with wiring and lighting, and you're set. When you want to leave work behind, simply close the doors. If you want the office chair to hide too, make the desk a little shallower.

Space under stairs often goes unused because it angles down to a height where a person can't stand up. But you may be able to tuck in a desk quite easily. The exact configuration will depend on whether the stairs go straight up or take a turn along the way. Whatever the plan, the interesting angles usually add to the charm of this type of workspace. See pages 20–21 for more ideas about how to add shelving under stairs.

On a long, straight run of stairs, a compact office fits directly underneath the treads. Track lights were added with a surface-wiring system. It has protective strips that allow you to attach wires to walls or ceilings without cutting into the drywall or plaster. In a confined space, such as a small room under stairs, cool-burning compact fluorescents would be an ideal choice.

Fitting an Office into a Closet

In many houses, the best place to add an office may be an empty closet. There are numerous ways to accomplish this. The simplest approach (below, left) calls for installing several built-in shelves, including one that serves as a desktop. In this version, the desk has a thin built-in drawer and the top shelf is fitted with sliding doors. In a wider cabinet (below, right) there is space for more substantial upper cabinets, as well as a lower cabinet that holds files. A third option (bottom) houses electronics in the cabinet but puts the desk on a table that faces into the room. All three plans let you close the doors when you want to leave work behind.

Multiuse offices

Besides converting a room or tucking a work area into a closet or other empty space, there's another way to create a home office: build one into a room that also serves another purpose. Prime locations include guest bedrooms, family rooms, dining rooms, and mudrooms.

A dining room may seem an unconventional place for an office, but if you tend to use the dining room only for holiday dinners, it could be the perfect location. With a little ingenuity, you could even add the office and still use the room for daily dining. One solution is to build the desk into a wall system that also serves as a china cabinet. Don't use the dining table as a desk—it's not the right height. The table should not be your main office storage area either, though it's a good place to spread out a project while you're working on it.

Recessed into a wall of built-in cabinets, a compact home office fits unobtrusively into a dining room.

A guest bedroom may be the best spot unless you tend to have long-term guests and work full time from home. To free up more room for the office area, consider building in a space-saving bed, either a pull-down Murphy bed or a window seat or couch with drawers underneath where you can store the bedding.

With electronics becoming more compact all the time, a simple cabinet set into a wall is all you need to create a mini office in a bedroom. The cabinet's door is hinged at the bottom, so it folds out to create the desk's top. A wired-in light keeps shadows away.

This home office and entertainment center includes a long desktop with a spacious open area underneath. There's plenty of room for several people to work at the same time, even in roomy office chairs.

ABOVE: A narrow table with a couple of built-in shelves converts a wide hallway or open wall into an office.

RIGHT: Bifold doors that slide in tracks above and below allow the homeowner to leave work behind at the end of the day, even though the office is at one end of the living room.

A family room lives up to its name when equipped with a home office. Kids can complete homework while parents are reading or attending to other tasks. When these roles are reversed, parents can work at computers while the kids watch TV or play board games. Either way, the setup helps parents monitor what's going on and puts family members in a place where they're more likely to interact.

BUILT-INS FOR OTHER AREAS

BUILT-INS MAKE GOOD USE OF SPACE that's cramped or awkward or that needs to have multiple uses. So it's no wonder that built-ins help transform a home's auxiliary rooms, such as entries, passageways, and laundry areas. Built-ins are also key components of most attic and basement conversions. Because they are inherently space efficient and because they are custom-designed to fit the spaces available, they excel in overcoming the challenges these rooms pose. Some of the possibilities:

- A BACK ENTRY with the right cabinets can function as both a laundry area and a mudroom yet not leave you embarrassed if a neighbor also comes into your house that way.
- A WIDE HALLWAY with recessed shelves in one or both walls becomes more than a mere travel route; it also functions as a library or a gallery for collectibles. In especially wide hallways or on stair landings, there may be enough room for a reading nook or a desk.
- A BASEMENT might seem difficult to use because heating ducts hang low on the ceiling. Strategically placed built-ins overcome this and allow the space to function as a family room, a pleasant laundry area, an office, or whatever else you need.

Built-ins create a gracious foyer where people would otherwise enter directly into the living room. The floor-to-ceiling section includes a coat closet topped with high cabinets for out-of-season items. It has a mirror on the side, a nice feature when you're headed out the door.

A compact gift-wrapping center squeezes into a small laundry area, thanks to a smart use of built-ins. The counter provides work space, while scissors, tape, and other supplies fit into the drawer below or the cabinets above.

LEFT: Built-ins can also accommodate pets. This entry bench gives the family dog a place to curl up. Drawers on either side have room for food and other pet supplies.

ABOVE: A few steps down from the entry of this house, a built-in cabinet contains a closet for coats. Underneath that, an open cubby holds a pad for the family dog.

LEFT: Built-in features that fit into walls give this entry its charm. A small display shelf tucks into one corner. The main wall has an open alcove above, which allows a view into the room beyond, as well as a short but wide alcove at the bottom, which helps keep shoes where no one will trip on them.

BELOW: Pullout shelves accessible from the sides make it easier to use all of the storage space under the stairs in this mudroom.

A bench and enclosed storage in drawers and baskets are nice additions to this entry setup. Large over-the-shoulder bags need about 30 inches of hanging space below a hook or a peg.

Cubbies for entries

Entries are the first stop in your home. They set the tone for what family members and visitors experience, so you want them tidy and welcoming. But spaces just inside the front and back doors also need to be storage areas. They serve as catchalls for shoes and keys, jackets and hats, and maybe junk mail or things that need to be delivered elsewhere the next time you run errands. Built-ins accommodate all this stuff and still leave a space looking neat.

If you have kids, you may have discovered that even opening the door to a coat closet may be too much for them to do when they're racing into the house. Cubbies equipped with pegs or hooks tend to work much better, which is why they are often used in built-ins, especially those near back doors. The appropriate size varies according to how the cubbies will be used. You also have options about how to combine them with other features, such as drawers or benches.

Low cubbies near a back door give kids a place to stash toys that are used outdoors. At the far end, the white panel serves both as a backrest for a bench and as a family message board. To create a message board like this, buy a panel designed specifically as a dry-erase board or use a melamine-coated panel sold as tile board at home centers and lumberyards (test the panel before you install it, to make sure marks wipe off).

FAR LEFT: Allow a height of 36 inches, or even more, to hang adult-size jackets from pegs or hooks. Two compact levels of storage will still fit underneath if you eliminate the usual toe-kick base.

LEFT: If you want people to stash their shoes out of the way as they enter, it shouldn't take many extra steps. A bench that is open underneath makes being neat almost effortless.

LEFT: Cubbies for backpacks can be tall and thin or short and thick. If you don't have much depth to work with, install hooks so backpacks don't tumble out. Allow about 24 inches for the packs to hang. If depth isn't a problem, skip the hooks and make the cubbies deeper so kids can just slide in their packs. Cubbies 18 inches deep and 12 to 15 inches tall, or vice versa, would work.

Laundry rooms

To create an efficient laundry room, you need places to wash, dry, fold, and maybe iron clothes, plus a way to store items that are headed into the wash or back to various bedrooms or closets. Kitchen designers think about how a chef moves between food preparation, cooking, and cleanup. A similar process pays off when you are designing a laundry room. Besides thinking through all the steps involved in doing laundry, also factor in any other special needs you have, such as a place to store vacuum cleaners, brooms, and spare household items such as light bulbs and paper towels.

As you plan built-ins, consider a sink which gives you a place to rinse away spills before stains set and to hand-launder delicate garments. It's also handy if you use the laundry room for crafts projects or watering houseplants. A sink with a single large bowl, rather than two or three small bowls, allows you to wash things that might not fit in your kitchen sink.

An island in a laundry-mudroom provides a place to fold and stack clothes. It also serves as a dock for a laundry cart that the homeowners wheel in from bedrooms. The design shields the mess from people coming and going through the home's back entry.

Another way to keep dirty clothes out of sight is to build hampers into laundry-room cabinets. A wire hamper allows air to circulate so clothes awaiting washing don't become musty.

The washer and dryer don't have to consist of the standard combination of a top-loading washer and a front-loading dryer. Other options work better with built-ins. Energy-efficient front-loading machines with controls on the face fit under a counter, giving you additional space for folding clothes. Many of these machines also stack. And there are combination washer-dryers, which have a dryer over a washer. With stacked units, the dryer opens at a comfortable height so you can fold garments as you remove them.

An island can be as useful in a laundry room as it is in a kitchen, provided the laundry area is big enough. An island adds storage and gives you a place to fold and stack clothes. If the laundry is by the back door, you might also want to use an island as a low room divider to shield the laundry area from the entry.

An ironing board can be built into a recessed cabinet so that it folds away when not in use. There are also built-in ironing boards that fold into a top drawer in base cabinets. But foldaway ironing boards cost more than freestanding types and can be used only in the room where they are installed. If you like to watch TV as you iron and don't have a TV in the laundry room, you might be happier with with a movable setup.

ABOVE, LEFT: Detergent and other supplies are within easy reach in this compact laundry, which is equipped with an energy-efficient front-loading washer and a matching dryer.

LEFT: When laundry time is over, everything goes into hiding behind doors. The top cabinet has pocket doors, which fold into the sides of the cabinets. The lower doors are mock drawer fronts, which have panels that match other cabinet components. These doors swing on standard hinges.

Stair landings

Although a staircase might seem like a small hallway, it actually occupies a two-story slice of a house because of the headroom it requires. Given the space commitment, it's nice if it serves a purpose other than just helping people up and down between floors. Built-ins can go alongside stairs or underneath, as shown in previous pages. But there are other opportunities as well.

● A STAIRCASE THAT TURNS turns often has a wide landing midway up. Besides making the geometry of the stairs work better, this flat area adds safety, as it breaks a long flight into shorter spans where someone isn't as likely to get seriously hurt in a fall. A landing also invites people to pause to catch their breath as they climb. Window seats or even small built-in offices make useful additions to landings.

● THE TOP OF A STAIRWAY often serves as a wide hallway to other rooms. Depending on how much space there is, you may be able to build in cabinets that create a laundry, an office, a guest room, or a play space.

Built-ins turn awkwardly shaped spaces into assets. On this stair landing, the display shelves and window seat fit into walls that are too low to be useable parts of rooms.

BELOW: A second-floor landing becomes a pleasant spot for reading with the addition of comfortable seating and built-in bookcases.

RIGHT: Tucked into the wall of a stair landing, this built-in bookcase and desk create a mini office. Because the work surface is attached to the wall, the desk needs no leg at the front. This frees people who sit at the desk to lean back in the chair and stretch out their legs.

TOP, LEFT: When windows face a landing, there may be space on either side for a bookcase. Here, an additional bookcase fits into a wall alongside the stairs.

TOP, RIGHT: Equipped with a daybed, a wide stair landing serves as a reading nook or guest quarters.

Kids can play in a wide spot in an upstairs hallway, out of the way of other activities in this small cottage. The open shelves are stocked with toys.

Passageways

There are a couple of reasons it often makes sense to add built-ins to passageways, which include hallways as well as places where one room opens directly into the next. One obvious benefit is the additional storage or display space. There's often a psychological benefit as well, because of the way built-ins warm a space and give it personality.

In hallways, use built-ins to bring life to long, dark spaces. Consider adding narrow shelves along one or both sides. If you want deeper shelves or cabinets, recess them into the wall or even go through the wall and borrow a little space from an adjoining room. Built-in display space works especially well in hallways because you get to enjoy the collectibles or art pieces as you go back and forth. Because hallways tend to be semiprivate spaces, they're good places for family pictures.

A hallway lined with dark wooden bookcases subtly heightens your interest in reaching the brighter room beyond. Most people experience a slight thrill when they pass from a dark space into one filled with light.

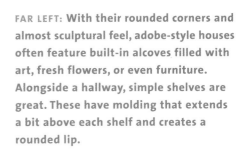

FAR LEFT: With their rounded corners and almost sculptural feel, adobe-style houses often feature built-in alcoves filled with art, fresh flowers, or even furniture. Alongside a hallway, simple shelves are great. These have molding that extends a bit above each shelf and creates a rounded lip.

LEFT: Where rooms don't have a hallway between them but you wish they did, built-in bookcases around the door do the trick. The setup here includes pocket doors, which the owners slide out when they want to completely close off the rooms.

Between rooms joined by only a doorway, use built-ins to more clearly define the separate spaces. By building in bookshelves that flank the door and extend above it, for example, you will subtly increase the apparent distance between the rooms. This, in turn, will increase their perceived separation and signal that by passing through you are leaving a public space and entering a private realm. This idea might be useful if you have a living room that leads directly into a bedroom, or perhaps an entry directly connected to a den where you want more seclusion.

BELOW: A hallway literally comes to life if you build in a fish tank, preferably one equipped with a light. This tank extends through the wall so people can enjoy it from both sides. The storage areas and display niches open only on one side; paneling fills in on the back.

LEFT: A recessed cabinet and display area brighten a hallway and make it more useful. A relatively deep cabinet like this uses the stud space within the wall and steals a little space from the adjoining room.

Up in the attic

If you decide to convert an attic into a bedroom, office, or teen hangout, built-ins will almost certainly allow you to make the most of the space. You can design them to fit better than furniture could into the angled areas under eaves. Before you settle on a plan, consider whether to add more natural light. You can design built-ins to work well with either skylights or dormers. For example, you might want to locate a desk under a skylight or build a window seat or bookshelves into a dormer.

ABOVE: **Built-in cabinets function like armoires, with hanging space above and drawers below. If the drawers were hidden behind doors, as in standard closets, they couldn't be as deep.**

RIGHT: **Lined with built-in bookcases, an attic hallway becomes a spacious library illuminated with skylights and ceiling fixtures.**

Case Study: Attic conversion

Attic conversions often pack multiple uses into a relatively small space. This house gained a home office and crafts room, guest beds, and a bathroom. At one end of the room (right), built-in bookshelves and cabinets follow the shape of the roof. Uplights hidden in the beams bounce light off the ceiling at night, when the skylights are dark. In the office and crafts area (bottom, right), a long, built-in desk extends across a low wall under the sharply pitched ceiling. Natural light through skylights is perfect for detail work. Toe-to-toe built-in beds (below) are elevated because they lie over a heating duct, a good example of the way built-ins can fit around room elements that pre-clude the use of standard furniture. Kids love the alcove ceiling, which makes the beds seem like they are in the cabin of a ship. True to the make-every-inch-count tradition of boatbuilding, shelves and drawers below the mattresses use space not occupied by the duct. These storage spaces hold toys, games, and books.

Built-ins fit nicely underneath ducts that run below ceiling height in a garage or basement. Bright colors create a cheery atmosphere in a space that doubles as a laundry and entertainment room.

Basements and garages

Just as with attic conversions, remodeling projects aimed at making better use of basements or garages often call for cleverly designed built-ins. But instead of trying to work around low, angled walls, you're more likely to confront low ducts, low ceilings, or equipment such as furnaces or water heaters. Plus, you may have to overcome a lack of natural light. Many garages lack windows, and basements often have only what fire-safety codes require so people can escape in an emergency.

If drainage problems plague a basement, fix them before you add insulation, drywall, flooring, or built-ins. Even so, if you fear that a leak might develop someday, design built-ins so they stay high and dry even if the floor becomes damp. You may need only one simple change: Instead of setting cabinets on a solid base, use metal legs or hang the cabinets on the walls.

A low duct that runs over a countertop slightly reduces overhead storage in this garage-turned-office, but that's not a huge drawback. There is plenty of space on the open shelves, in base cabinets, and on the stand-alone desk.

Colorful cabinets and inexpensive indoor-outdoor carpeting convert a garage into a play space yet make it easy to reconvert when the kids grow up or it's time to sell. If you design built-ins so they don't interfere with parking, they can stay regardless of how you use the rest of the space. Indoor-outdoor carpet works especially well over concrete garage floors and in basements because it's unlikely to mildew if it gets wet.

Windows that create a ribbon of light are a bright addition to a basement that's been converted into living space. Here, a pull-down bed allows the room to become a guest bedroom.

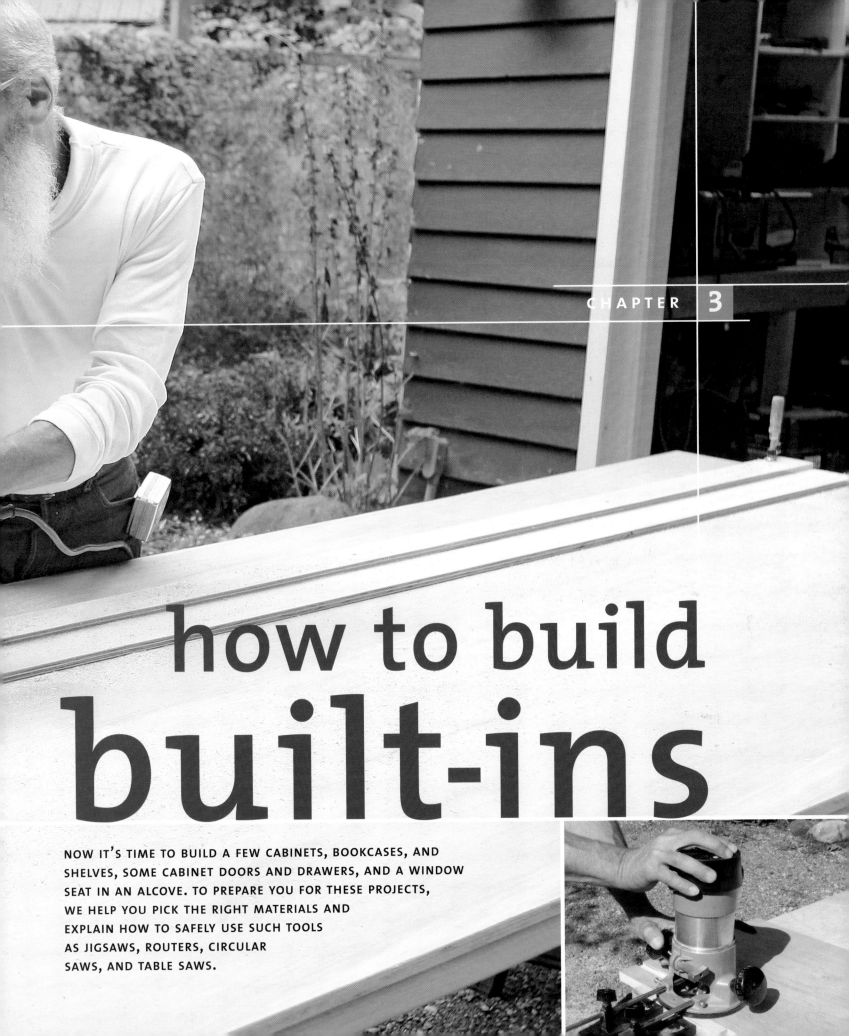

how to build
built-ins

NOW IT'S TIME TO BUILD A FEW CABINETS, BOOKCASES, AND
SHELVES, SOME CABINET DOORS AND DRAWERS, AND A WINDOW
SEAT IN AN ALCOVE. TO PREPARE YOU FOR THESE PROJECTS,
WE HELP YOU PICK THE RIGHT MATERIALS AND
EXPLAIN HOW TO SAFELY USE SUCH TOOLS
AS JIGSAWS, ROUTERS, CIRCULAR
SAWS, AND TABLE SAWS.

BUILDING FROM SCRATCH

CREATING A BUILT-IN FROM SCRATCH may seem intimidating at first, but if you break the project into its most basic elements, it's likely to look more feasible. After all, most built-ins are essentially just shelves, boxes, or combinations thereof. Whether you tackle the construction yourself or hire a carpenter, building from scratch gives you maximum flexibility in design and materials. Choosing the dimensions, finishes, and hardware is all up to you.

If you do the work yourself, match the project to your skill level and available tools. Simple built-ins that are well made are much more satisfying to live with than elaborate projects with miter joints that aren't tight and drawers that don't quite fit. If some components, such as those troublesome drawers, will take more time than you are able to devote to the project, consider buying those pieces ready-made (see pages 138–141).

A built-in closet and a low chest that doubles as a small bureau and a nightstand show how beautiful boxes can be. The tall one on the right is fitted with doors, shelves, and a rod for hanging clothes. The other is equipped with drawers, which are also boxes. Steps to make all of these components are shown on the following pages: the cabinet boxes (pages 198–202); shelves with edging (page 169); and drawers (pages 212–215). See page 216 for tips on installing a recessed base.

Only simple tools are needed to build a bench like this. Add cushions over the storage cubbies and you have a comfortable spot for kids to do homework while parents are preparing dinner. This bench consists of boxes set on toe-kick bases (page 216), then topped with a seat scribed to fit snugly against the walls (page 175).

LEFT: One step up from the kitchen, this breakfast nook offers diners views out a side window. The benches are made of two boxes like the bookcases on pages 190–191. The table is attached to the wall at one end and held up by a wide leg in the middle, which saves space and makes the nook easy to clean.

BELOW: A bookcase is a terrific project for a woodworker who's never tackled a built-in before. The steps include measuring the space (page 166), building two cabinet boxes (pages 190–191), installing them on toe-kick bases (page 216), and finishing it all with molding (pages 218–221).

Using ready-made pieces

You don't need to create built-ins entirely from scratch in order to achieve a custom look. You can also make them out of ready-made components such as cabinets, which can be purchased new or used. Other pieces you can order include doors and drawers.

The biggest challenge is finding the right combination of elements for your project. This is because stock cabinets come in set sizes, which differ according to whether the cabinets are designed for kitchens, bathrooms, or offices. But you don't need to stick with the standard uses. You can use cabinets sized for one room in another, and you can orient cabinets in unconventional ways. For example:

• MAKE A SECRETARY-STYLE DESK with a fold-down writing surface by tipping a wall cabinet with a single swinging door on its side onto a base cabinet that's set on a toe-kick base. Add lid-support hinges to the door, and reorient the shelves of the wall cabinet to create horizontal surfaces.

• GET A WORKING DRAWER in a sink cabinet by foregoing a standard vanity, which has a false drawer front covering space needed for the sink and plumbing. Instead, buy an inverted frame cabinet. Upside down relative to the standard configuration, this kind of cabinet has a drawer at the bottom, away from the plumbing.

Kitchen designers know which sizes and features are available, so these specialists can help you select cabinets for your project. If you shop from a catalog or Web site, avoid confusion by noting the code identifying each model. The first letter or

Ready-made cabinets that are designed for kitchens typically have a recessed toe-kick, but ones for other rooms, such as this home office, incorporate baseboard molding for a more formal look.

letters indicate the cabinet type: W for wall, B for base, V for vanity, VS for vanity sink cabinet, etc. Then come numbers, the first one or two for width in inches, then one or two for height in inches. Fractions are shown with decimals. Letters at the end describe features. BD, for example, means "butt doors" hinged on the sides.

ABOVE: Stock cabinets can be combined to mimic the look of a custom-made built-in that features spacious shelves and a comfortable window seat. For example, the bookcases on either side of the windows above this cushioned seat could be made of ready-made wall cabinets. Similarly, the drawers below the window seat could be made from what cabinet manufacturers call furniture drawers, which are sold individually. Ones 12 inches wide and 15 inches high would work well here. For the toe-kick drawers, you could purchase a pair of furniture drawers 30 inches wide by 6 inches high.

Choosing cabinets

Factory-made cabinets come in a variety of sizes geared to what people typically want in common locations. For example, modern kitchen base cabinets are 24 inches deep because that dimension accommodates dishwashers and sinks. But base cabinets labeled as vanities are just 18 or 21 inches deep, as bathroom sinks are smaller and floor space is often tight. Base units made for offices are shorter than other types to provide a comfortable countertop height for someone in a chair. It's fine to combine components made for different rooms.

Besides the basic wall and base cabinets, consider some lesser-known cabinets that are especially useful for built-ins:

• DRAWER BOXES, which have one or more drawers housed in a box, can be stacked or installed like wall cabinets. Buy different sizes and stack them like Japanese tansu under stairs. Or get several of one size and use them as benches in mudrooms or as window seats. Desk drawer boxes are designed to fit between cabinets and support a countertop, thus turning a gap between cabinets into a desk. Spice-drawer cabinets for walls are shallow and can be installed vertically or horizontally.

• ORGANIZERS are short, shallow wall cabinets with compartments of different sizes. Designed to function like the cubbyhole spaces on a rolltop desk, they're usually installed horizontally. You can also tip the cabinets and install them vertically, turning the trays for paper into dividers that hold magazines upright.

Built-ins should be efficient, but don't try to fit cabinets tight against sidewalls or the ceiling. Leave a gap of at least $\frac{1}{2}$ inch on each side so you can maneuver the cabinets into place. If cabinets have full-overlay doors (see pages 206–211), allow at least 1 inch. If you are tilting floor-to-ceiling cabinets into place, you will need an even larger gap depending on the depth of the cabinet (measure diagonally to calculate maximum tilting height). Or, better yet, install several shorter cabinets stacked on top of each other. Cover the gaps between cabinets and walls with filler strips.

TOP: **Though usually called spice drawers, the smallest stock cabinet drawers have many uses, from storing yarn or other crafts materials to holding bathroom toiletries.**

RIGHT: **A pantry closet with pullout shelves works as well in a crafts room as it does in a kitchen. Though originally designed to hold serving trays and cookie sheets, the vertical dividers at the top provide good storage for poster board and other large paper materials.**

Sizing Stock Cabinets

Although it's sometimes possible to modify stock cabinets to make them work in a built-in, it's far easier to buy components that fit a space as is. Here's a quick rundown of common sizes. Manufacturer specs may vary.

*Dimensions typically increase in 3-inch increments within the range listed.

WALL CABINET

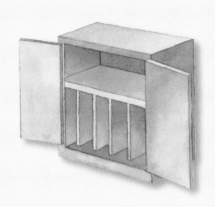

DIMENSIONS

H: 9–48*

W: 12–42*

D: 12

USES
- Upper cabinet
- Wall-mounted bookshelf
- Shallow base cabinet
- Room divider

KITCHEN BASE CABINET

DIMENSIONS

H: 34$^1/_2$

W: 9–48*

D: 24

USES
- Stand-alone base cabinet
- Island
- Countertop for use while standing or seated on a bar stool

VANITY BASE CABINET

DIMENSIONS

H: 33$^1/_2$

W: 9–60*

D: 18 or 21

USES
- Base cabinet below shallow countertop
- Base cabinet below slightly lower countertop

DESK BASE CABINET

DIMENSIONS

H: 29

W: 9–48*

D: 24

USES
- Base cabinet for chair-based work
- Buy several and combine with wall cabinets for a wall system

TALL CABINET

DIMENSIONS

H: 84, 90, or 96

W: 9–36*

D: 12–24*

USES
- Pantry
- Utility cabinet
- Bookcase
- Crafts center

A hybrid approach

In some cases, it makes sense to build some parts of your built-in from scratch and purchase others ready-made or as ready-to-assemble units. You can buy everything from cabinet boxes and shelves to drawers and doors. Find components at home centers and lumber-yards, or order from a factory. Some suppliers deal only with professionals, while others sell in small quantities to anyone. The Resources section in the back of this book lists several sources. Also look on the internet for additional suppliers in your area. Stores that specialize in used building materials are another option, but their inventory is limited to whatever they happen to take in as salvage.

If you need an entire suite of cabinets, ordering everything as components may save little, if any, money, especially if you hire someone to do the installation. However, you may be able to save quite a lot with a hybrid approach: Make the cabinet boxes and shelves on your own but order the doors and drawers ready-made. Doors and drawers are the most challenging parts of a built-in to create with only simple tools, so ordering them as components helps ensure a top-quality result.

A built-in wine and storage cabinet (right) between the kitchen and the dining room of a condo is custom designed and mostly custom built. But the drawer fronts are from Ikea, so they match the nearby kitchen cabinetry (above).

ABOVE, LEFT: **Fronted by two pairs of distinctive glass doors, these otherwise simple cabinet boxes become an elegant built-in for a mudroom and pantry.**

ABOVE, RIGHT: **Stores that specialize in used building materials often carry wood-frame glass doors suitable for use on cabinets. Once you have your doors, you can build the cabinet to fit.**

RIGHT: **Even with simple tools, a weekend wood-worker could create a wall of built-ins like this by building the cabinet boxes and shelves from scratch and adding ready-made doors and drawers.**

Choosing Materials

WOOD IS THE STARTING POINT FOR MOST BUILT-INS. Choices range from solid softwoods and hardwoods to numerous kinds of plywood and particleboard (see pages 148–149), some of which have finishes or veneers already applied. For many projects, it makes sense to make some parts of your built-in from plywood or particleboard and other parts from solid wood.

SOFTWOOD LUMBER SIZES		
1 × 2	=	$^3/_4$" × $1^1/_2$"
1 × 3	=	$^3/_4$" × $2^1/_2$"
1 × 4	=	$^3/_4$" × $3^1/_2$"
1 × 6	=	$^3/_4$" × $5^1/_2$"
1 × 8	=	$^3/_4$" × $7^1/_4$"
1 × 10	=	$^3/_4$" × $9^1/_4$"
1 × 12	=	$^3/_4$" × $11^1/_4$"
2 × 2	=	$1^1/_2$" × $1^1/_2$"
2 × 4	=	$1^1/_2$" × $3^1/_2$"

Softwood is normally sold in lengths ranging from 6 to 20 feet, in increments of 2 feet.

Using solid wood

Solid wood has a natural, honest look that you don't have to hide behind edging or veneers. If a piece chips, the result is the patina of age rather than a frayed edge, as would be the case with, say, particleboard. That's why solid wood is generally the best choice for components with numerous exposed edges that are subject to wear, such as face frames (the decorative bands that cover the front of cabinet boxes) and the frames of cabinet doors. Solid wood is also a practical choice if you are working with handsaws, which tend to choke on the crisscross fibers in plywood and quickly dull from encounters with the resin in particleboard.

Because solid wood is a natural product, no two pieces are identical. Besides obvious differences like color and the location of knots, boards can vary depending on the way in which they were sliced from a log. Changes in humidity can cause wood to expand and contract, which in turn can cause joints to open up, even if they fit perfectly at first. Solid wood can also cup or develop deep cracks, known as checks.

Softwoods, which are harvested from conifers, include pine, fir, redwood, and cedar. These are generally less expensive, easier to tool, and more readily available than hardwoods. However, clear or knot-free softwood boards are rare today and may cost more than some clear hardwoods.

Home centers and lumberyards sell softwood that is smooth on all four sides. The measurements used to describe the boards aren't their actual sizes. Rather, they refer to the size of the wood when it was freshly cut. Drying causes the boards to shrink, and more wood disappears when the rough fibers left over from sawing are shaved smooth in

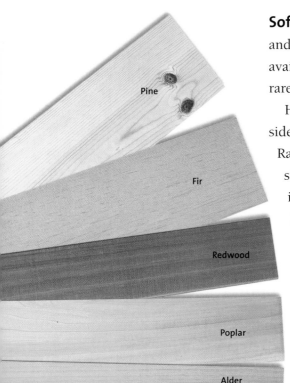

Pine

Fir

Redwood

Poplar

Alder

DID YOU KNOW?

Woods classified as hardwoods tend to be denser than softwoods, but some are still quite soft. Poplar and alder, for example, are hardwoods that dent about as easily as pine, fir, and redwood, which is why they are sometimes lumped in with softwoods.

Walnut

Mahogany

Maple

Cherry

Birch

Oak

a planer. A so-called 1 × 2 piece of fir is actually only ³/₄ inch thick and 1¹/₂ inches wide (see chart on opposite page). Labeled lengths do reflect actual board lengths.

Lumberyards usually sell softwood lumber by the linear foot, while home centers tend to sell it by the piece. For example, at a lumberyard, you might ask for 40 linear feet of 1 × 10 boards. That would be the same amount of wood that you'd get at a home center if you picked out five boards from a display of 1 × 10s that are each 8 feet long.

Hardwoods come mostly from deciduous trees and occasionally from broad-leaf evergreens, such as madrone. Popular types for built-ins include white and red oak, cherry, maple, birch, walnut, alder, mahogany, and poplar. If you want a natural finish on a built-in, you might choose a wood simply based on its appearance. However, there are also practical issues involved.

• PAINTABILITY Poplar is a particularly good choice for built-ins that you plan to paint. Knot-free boards are easy to find, relatively inexpensive, and easy to shape and sand, because the wood is quite soft for a hardwood. Poplar boards often have a greenish tinge that many people find unappealing, but paint covers it nicely.

• STRENGTH Oak and maple can span longer distances without sagging than shelves made of plywood, particleboard, or some of the other hardwoods, assuming the materials are equally thick (see chart, page 168). Sag resistance alone might be a reason to choose oak or maple for wide bookshelves where you want a sleek design without vertical supports. Oak staircase treads are a good option for shelves because they are thicker than standard boards and have a rounded edge on one side. Treads made from other woods also work, but they aren't as common.

• STABILITY Maple tends to expand and contract across its width more than most other common hardwoods. If you are building door frames or other parts that must fit precisely, use narrow pieces of maple rather than wide ones.

• APPEARANCE Birch, maple, and oak are the hardwoods most often used for the face (exterior) surfaces in hardwood plywood, as well as for iron-on veneer tape, which you can use to cover edges of plywood and particleboard. If you are planning a project that incorporates both solid and plywood pieces of these woods and you want to use a clear finish, line up all of the pieces before you buy them, or you might be stuck with contrasts and variations you don't want.

BY THE NUMBERS

Hardwood lumber tends to be slightly thicker than softwood lumber that's advertised as being the same thickness, so always measure before you start to build. For example, boards that you expect to be ³/₄ (or ¹²/₁₆) inch thick might actually be ¹³/₁₆ inch thick, which could be the difference between a drawer opening smoothly or not.

Lumberyards typically sell hardwood lumber by the board foot, a volume measurement equal to wood that's 1 inch thick and 12 inches long and wide. Volume is the most convenient measure at these stores because they stock hardwood boards in random widths and lengths, and with rough edges that aren't necessarily straight. This minimizes waste but adds to the amount of processing you need to do once you take the boards home. To make hardwood lumber easier to use, some home centers and specialty lumberyards now sell it smooth on all four sides and in set lengths. If you have only a few tools, this is the way to buy hardwood.

The thickness of hardwood lumber may be expressed in inches, just as with softwood lumber, or you may hear salespeople refer to "five-four" or "four-four." The 4 at the end signals that the first number refers to fourths of an inch, so five-four boards were 1¼ inches thick when first cut and are usually down to about 1 inch thick when you use them. The four-four boards were sliced 1 inch thick and go to about ¾ inch once they are dry and smooth.

ABOVE: **Solid wood, rather than sheet material, is the right choice for framing doors like these; it's also used for paneling in this built-in closet and for the trim that ties the closet to the rest of the room.**

SHOPPING TIP

Home centers and lumberyards sometimes carry wide panels made of thin boards glued together. They're good time savers for projects that require wide pieces of solid wood, but check the end grain, as you would on individual boards, so you don't wind up with pieces that split or curl.

RIGHT: **Specialty lumberyards carry exotic tropical woods with intriguing colors or grain patterns. Some species have been heavily logged, so the wood is increasingly rare and expensive. If you do decide to work with these woods, consider using veneers, which make better use of the scarce resource, and look for wood certified by the Forest Stewardship Council (www.fscus.org). The sawdust of many exotic tropical woods can trigger allergic reactions, so wear a respirator when you saw or sand.**

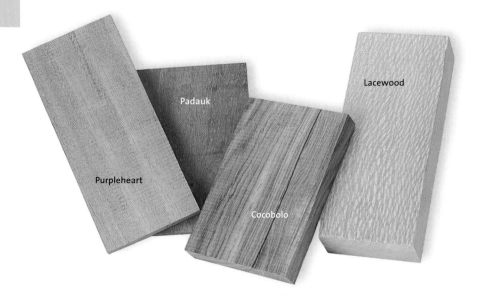

Lacewood

Padauk

Purpleheart

Cocobolo

Shopping for wood

There's more to buying a good board than looking for a grain pattern you like. The board also needs to be straight and not prone to splitting or cupping. Check for a crook by looking lengthwise down the flat side of a board, or a bow, which you can spot by peering lengthwise down its edge; they might not matter if you'll be cutting the board into small lengths. Also check the end of the board to inspect the growth rings. Their orientation varies depending on how the board was cut from a log, as shown in the illustration below. In general, vertical-grain lumber is less likely to cup or twist than flat-grain lumber. Here are a few things to keep in mind:

• GROWTH RINGS THAT RUN UP AND DOWN or at a uniform angle are the mark of a board that is likely to remain straight across its width. Save these boards for the most important parts of your project.

• GROWTH RINGS THAT CURL UP in a smile or down in a frown are a sign of a board that will cup in the direction opposite to the way the rings bend.

• A DARK CIRCLE is a tip that the board is likely to split. Wood on either side of the circle (once the center of a tree) is fine, though, so by cutting out the center and gluing the remaining pieces back together, you can create boards that will remain solid and straight.

FROM TREE TO BOARD

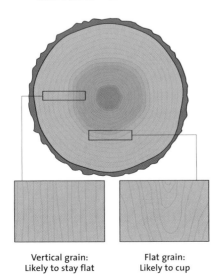

Vertical grain:
Likely to stay flat

Flat grain:
Likely to cup

CUPPED BOARDS

Though these boards were flat when milled, they now cup enough to create a visible gap at the center when they are placed on top of each other. The annual growth rings, visible on the ends, tend to straighten out as the wood dries, so the cup winds up in the opposite direction from the ring orientation.

CUT OUT THE CENTER

The board on the right contains a bull's eye of dark wood, which was once the center of the tree. If you rip a board with this kind of grain, you can wind up with a piece like that on the left that has a straight grain, which means the growth rings run nearly straight up and down across the board's width.

STRAIGHT GRAINS MEAN FLAT BOARDS

Woodworkers prize straight-grain wood because it doesn't cup. Wide pieces of straight-grain lumber are hard to find these days because they come from big, old trees. For wide boards that stay flat, glue narrow pieces edge to edge.

Sheet products

Plywood and particleboard offer several advantages over solid wood. They come in large sheets, tend to remain flat and stable, and usually cost less than the same amount of wood purchased as boards. However, you'll probably need to mask at least the edges with veneers or strips of solid wood if you want to create built-ins with a clear finish and a traditional look.

The outermost layers of plywood have a distinct grain, which runs in the long dimension of a sheet. Cut shelves and most other parts to follow this grain. This orientation usually looks better, as it mimics the look of solid wood. Plus, it's the direction in which the plywood has the most strength and sag resistance, because more of its layers run that way. Particleboard, medium-density fiberboard (MDF), and hardboard don't have a grain, so you can cut pieces to minimize waste.

Plywood is the staple of most built-ins. Standard veneer-core plywood has an odd number of thin wood layers, which were peeled from a log and glued together. Except for specialty plywood made to form curved surfaces, the grain of each veneer runs perpendicular to the layers above and below. This makes plywood strong and stable in all directions, though plywood with only a few layers still tends to curl somewhat. Standard sheets measure 4 by 8 feet, although some hardwood plywood is 1 inch wider and longer to allow for trimming. Thicknesses range from $\frac{1}{4}$ to $1\frac{1}{8}$ inches. If you need something thinner, ask for door-skin material, which is just $\frac{1}{8}$ inch thick.

• SOFTWOOD PLYWOOD is made mostly for construction of buildings, but it's also useful for built-ins. Types are described by letters that indicate the quality of the outside veneers. A/B, for example, has an A-quality veneer, which is smooth and paintable, on one side, and a B-quality veneer, with more patches, on the other. CDX has C and D faces, which have larger knots and splits. The X signals that the resin is waterproof, so the plywood is suitable for exterior use.

• HARDWOOD PLYWOOD is graded differently, with AA representing the highest-quality face veneer and E representing the lowest. Hardwood plywood usually has a core of hardwood veneers, but some sheets are based on particleboard, MDF, or a combination of two layers of MDF separated by a layer of veneer. Particleboard and MDF help panels stay flatter but add weight. A $\frac{3}{4}$-inch-thick sheet with one of these at the center weighs about 100 pounds, versus 60 to 70 pounds for veneer-core plywood.

Even when the face veneers on two sheets of plywood are the same, you may discover a significant price difference. The less expensive sheet, called "shop" or "paint grade," might have a top face with dark streaks and interior layers with a lot of voids where knots were. The other sheet might have a more uniform color and interior plies with fewer voids, making it a little stronger and more suitable for a clear finish.

Where you want extra-straight thin pieces with void-free edges, perhaps for drawer sides, use plywood made of numerous thin veneers, often sold as Baltic or Finnish birch or ApplePly.

A/C Fir Plywood   Oak Plywood   "Shop" Maple Plywood   Finnish Birch Plywood

Particleboard, which is sometimes called chipboard, is made from slivers of wood that are bonded together with resin. Like plywood, it's usually sold in 4-by-8-foot sheets, though home centers may also carry smaller sizes.

Particleboard is inexpensive and widely available. However, it isn't suitable for projects that might get wet, because the material swells and becomes permanently misshapen if it becomes damp. Particleboard is heavy and prone to sagging if it spans long distances (see page 168), and it doesn't grip well to nails or screws.

Medium-density fiberboard, usually called MDF, is a smoother, denser cousin of standard particleboard. Instead of consisting of slivers of wood, it's made from wood material that has been broken down even further, into individual fibers. This gives it a more homogeneous consistency, so pieces stay flatter and paint sticks better. The edges are dense enough so you can shape them with a router. MDF has more resin than other sheet materials, so it dulls tools faster and weighs more. Cutting and shaping it will kick up so much dust that even if you normally ignore advice about wearing a disposable respirator, you're likely to want one if you work with MDF.

Melamine is technically just a plastic coating applied at the factory, but the term is often used alone as a shorthand for melamine-coated particleboard. Widely available and popular for shelves and cabinet boxes, this material is sold in 4-by-8-foot sheets, usually $3/4$ inch thick. Lumberyards and home centers also carry narrow pieces precut for use as shelves and uprights. The uprights are predrilled for shelf pins.

One advantage of using melamine-coated material is that it needs no sanding or finishing. You just cover the edge with wood or iron-on veneer tape, perhaps one that matches the color of the melamine. White and almond are the most common colors, and you may be able to special-order a few others. A melamine finish resists staining from many spills, so it's great for shelves and cabinet interiors. It isn't waterproof or durable enough for countertops, though. For that, it's better to glue high-pressure laminate to standard particleboard, MDF, or plywood.

Hardboard is a high-density type of particleboard made from highly compressed wood fibers. It's commonly available in two thicknesses, $1/8$ and $1/4$ inch, in 4-by-8-foot sheets, and sometimes in smaller pieces. For built-ins, hardboard is used primarily for bookcase and cabinet backs and for drawer bottoms. Because it's inexpensive, it's also a good material for templates. Standard hardboard is easily painted and makes a superb base for blackboard paint, in case you want to incorporate that feature into doors, cabinet sides, or other elements of built-ins.

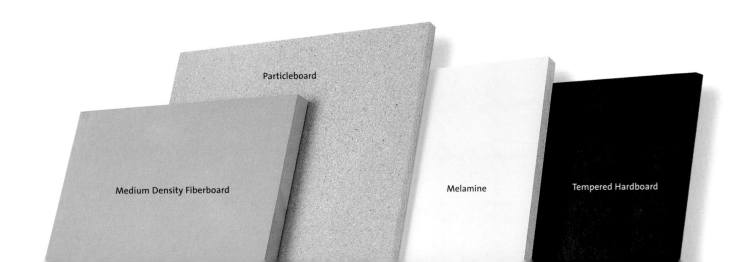

Particleboard

Medium Density Fiberboard

Melamine

Tempered Hardboard

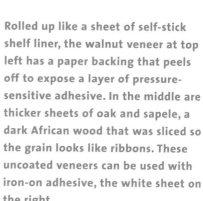

Veneers and laminates

With wood veneer or high-pressure plastic laminate, you can create your own custom-made sheet products for built-ins. Veneers transform standard particleboard or MDF into panels that look and feel like they are made of expensive wood, while plastic laminate makes surfaces colorful, water resistant, and durable.

Veneer is true wood, sliced $1/28$ inch thick or even thinner. Rotary veneer, which comes in wide pieces, is made of a thin layer of wood peeled from a log as it rotates on a lathe. This type has bold grain with lots of variation. Most other types of veneer are sliced from a log in sheets so they wind up with grain patterns similar to those you'd find in solid wood. Burl veneer is cut from the rounded growths that sometimes appear on tree trunks or branches. This wood is highly figured.

Cabinet shops that tackle large veneering projects use specialized equipment, such as vacuum presses. In home workshops, small projects often turn out best. For example, you might want to use burl veneer on door panels in a cabinet that consists mostly of solid wood or standard plywood. Shop for veneer at stores that specialize in woodworking supplies or hardwood lumber.

Some veneer products are made entirely of wood, while others have a paper backing or are coated on the back with pressure-sensitive or iron-on adhesive. Manufacturers also make wood veneer laminated to several layers of resin-impregnated brown paper, which makes the installation as easy as that of high-pressure laminate.

High-pressure laminate This material consists of a decorative paper layer sandwiched between a resin-impregnated brown paper base and a clear melamine top sheet. Manufacturers bond the layers with pressure and heat, and the result is a stiff sheet that can be glued with contact cement to particleboard or MDF (or plywood, though manufacturers may not recommend it). Hundreds of colors and patterns are available, some of which are photographs of natural wood or stone, while others are whimsical designs or solid colors. Laminate resists stains, and most spills wipe up easily.

Rolled up like a sheet of self-stick shelf liner, the walnut veneer at top left has a paper backing that peels off to expose a layer of pressure-sensitive adhesive. In the middle are thicker sheets of oak and sapele, a dark African wood that was sliced so the grain looks like ribbons. These uncoated veneers can be used with iron-on adhesive, the white sheet on the right.

SAFETY TIP

If you are concerned about exposure to formaldehyde, a pungent-smelling gas that can trigger asthma attacks and perhaps cause cancer, search for sheet materials made with formaldehyde-free resin. Or use softwood plywood with a grading stamp that includes the trademark "APA—The Engineered Wood Association." Made for exterior use, this plywood contains phenol-formaldehyde resin, which tends to stay locked within the wood. Most hardwood plywood, particleboard, and medium-density fiberboard (MDF) contain urea-formaldehyde resin, which releases formaldehyde into the air. MDF usually emits the highest amount.

The sapele veneer in this bathroom has a pommele figure. A French word meaning dappled, pommele refers to a pattern of rings that circle around each other. Pommele figure is usually found only in extremely large trees of a few African species, so veneer is the most economical and environmentally responsible way to enjoy it.

THE TOOLS YOU'LL NEED

ALTHOUGH MANY BUILT-INS ARE BORN in well-equipped cabinet shops, others are forged in modest home workshops with just a few key tools. If you are a home woodworker, the trick is to choose a project that is suited to your skills, tools, and time. A simple project that's well executed is much more satisfying than a complex one whose joints don't quite meet up. Even worse is the overly ambitious project that's started but never finished.

Many of the projects in this book require only two power tools: a drill (cordless or corded) and either a circular saw or a jigsaw. A handsaw isn't sufficient if you will be cutting plywood, particleboard, or MDF. You'll also need an assortment of hand tools, such as a square, a chalk line, and a hammer. Other power tools—a sander, a biscuit joiner, a table saw, and a router—will give your work a more professional look and can help you tackle more complicated projects.

This handsome room divider and shelf unit is easy to build with just a few basic tools.

About jigsaws

A jigsaw, also called a saber saw, is not a conventional tool for cabinetmaking, but it's a good choice for simple projects if you are inexperienced with power tools or you're planning to have your children help. A jigsaw does exactly what you expect—it cuts through wood as you move it forward. This is in contrast to a circular saw, which can hurl itself back at you unexpectedly if it binds in a board, or a table saw, which can do the same thing to a piece of wood if you have failed to support it properly. In addition to being relatively safe, a jigsaw is also versatile. Designed for cutting curves, it can also cut straight lines if you guide the saw against a straightedge. Of course, jigsaws can't do everything. You can't set the blade to a certain depth to cut a groove, as you can on a circular or table saw, and jigsaw cuts will never be as perfectly square. So while you can build a basic bookcase or a window seat with a jigsaw, you wouldn't want to tackle a frame-and-panel door, which features prominently exposed joints. Bottom line, if you plan to make a jigsaw your only power saw, invest in a good one.

High-quality jigsaws offer adjustments that inexpensive saws often lack. This saw has a base plate that tilts so you can make bevel cuts. There is a blower that you can switch on when you are cutting wood so that sawdust doesn't obscure the line. If you are cutting metal, turn off the blower. The blade's speed and orbital action, or sideways motion, are also adjustable. A saw with no sideways motion cuts a finer line, but a wider path results in a faster cut.

Cutting with a jigsaw

Besides the obvious safety issues, such as wearing protective eyewear and keeping fingers away from the blade, there are a few other tips that ensure good results.

• **SECURE THE PIECE** you are cutting to a work surface with two clamps. Using only one clamp creates a pivot point, which means the wood could move while you are cutting it.

• **ORIENT THE PIECE** so you won't accidentally cut into your work surface or saw through the cord.

• **TURN ON THE SAW** with its base planted firmly on the piece, but keep the blade's teeth away from the wood upon start-up or the saw is likely to jerk.

• **MOVE THE BLADE** into the wood with only enough pressure to keep the blade cutting steadily. Don't force the saw. Keep the base flat against the work.

• **CUT CURVES** with a narrow blade. If the curve is especially tight, the blade will need to carve out space so it can round the curve, so advance the saw slowly. If you try to force the saw into rounding a curve too fast, the blade is likely to angle out and you will wind up with a slanted edge.

• **CUT STRAIGHT LINES** with a wide blade, and guide the saw's base against a straightedge, or fence, clamped to the piece you are cutting. Keep the saw moving forward, though, as too much sideways pressure against the fence can force the blade to bend, especially if you are cutting through thick wood.

• **CUT CRISP INSIDE CORNERS** by tackling them in steps. First, cut to a corner and stop. Back the saw up and cut forward again, but this time round the corner with a curving pass that joins the line at a right angle to the corner. Now turn the saw off, lift it out of the channel it has just cut, turn it around, reinsert it into the channel, and head back into the corner to complete the cut.

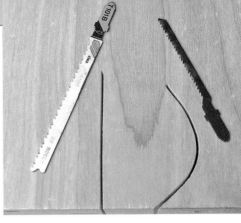

Fit a jigsaw with a wide blade (left) for straight cuts. Use a skinny blade (right) for curved cuts. Most jigsaw blades cut on the upstroke. That means the cut on the wood's top surface is rougher than it is on the bottom. If the top surface will be visible, mark the back and cut with that surface facing up.

To make a crisp inside corner with a jigsaw, make two straight cuts at a right angle to each other.

Straightedge with a Jigsaw

If you are cutting straight lines with a jigsaw, spend a couple of minutes making two spacers that show how much distance to leave between a line you want to cut and the straightedge that you'll use as a guide. Cut the spacers so they match the distance between the edge of the saw's base and the blade. Place the spacers at the beginning and end of the line you want to cut and you'll instantly see where to clamp the straightedge. The spacers show the distance between the saw's base and the outside edge of the blade, so place them and the straightedge on the piece you are making, not over the waste part.

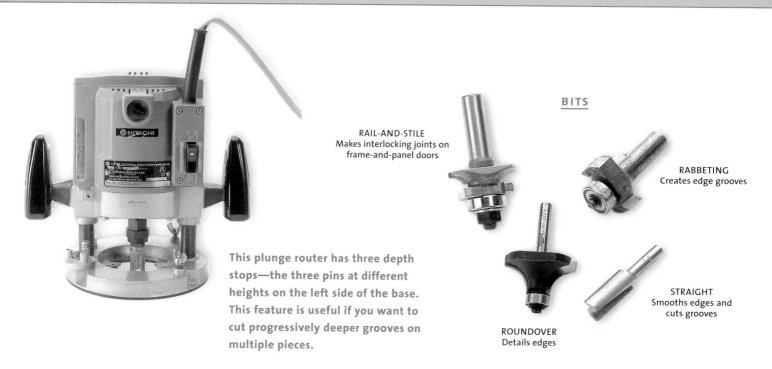

BITS

RAIL-AND-STILE
Makes interlocking joints on
frame-and-panel doors

RABBETING
Creates edge grooves

STRAIGHT
Smooths edges and
cuts grooves

ROUNDOVER
Details edges

This plunge router has three depth
stops—the three pins at different
heights on the left side of the base.
This feature is useful if you want to
cut progressively deeper grooves on
multiple pieces.

Using a router

This tool is so versatile that whole books have been written about it. Routers plow
grooves, shape edges, cut joints, and trim pieces so they match perfectly. With the right
bits, you can cut grooves for shelf standards, carve decorative coves or beads into the
edges of shelf boards, make raised-panel cabinet doors, and cut dovetails for drawers.

There are two basic kinds of routers: plunge and standard. A standard router has a bit
that's fixed at the depth you set. A plunge router has a spring mechanism that lowers or
retracts the bit depending on whether you press or relax pressure on the machine. If you
plan to use a router table (a necessity for cutting joints), get a standard type. A plunge
router is best if you want to do decorative designs that require you to begin cutting in the
middle of a board. Some manufacturers make routers with interchangeable bases that
allow you to use one machine in both ways.

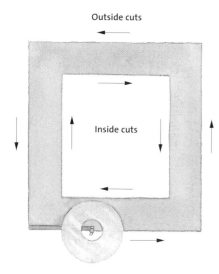

Outside cuts

Inside cuts

Because a router can be used right side up or upside
down, it's sometimes difficult to keep track of the
direction to run it on the piece of wood you are shaping. When a router is held right side up, its bit turns
clockwise, so make sure the bit is biting into the wood
at 9 o'clock. For example, if you are moving a router
forward along the edge of a piece of MDF to create a
rabbet joint, the MDF should be on your left. When a
router is mounted upside down in a router table, the
bit will be spinning counterclockwise. But because the
router is stationary and the board is now moving forward, the MDF should still be positioned to the left of
the spinning bit.

Cutting with a circular saw

A circular saw excels at cutting straight lines. Because it has a wider base and a stiffer, larger blade than a jigsaw, it also produces edges that are more reliably square. This makes it the better tool for advanced built-in projects that require sharp right angles. The key to working safely and accurately with a circular saw is preparation.

• CLAMP ALL PIECES, especially small ones, so they don't wiggle as you cut them.

• SUPPORT PANELS adequately so the kerf, or blade-wide line you are cutting, does not close up and bind the blade. That could cause the saw to jerk back, a situation known as kickback. Support thin material close to the cut line so the weight of the saw doesn't bend the wood and cause it to bind the blade. It's okay to let small pieces fall to the floor as you cut, but keep large pieces from dropping in mid-cut. If you enlist a person to help, make sure he or she doesn't lift the cut-off material upward. That could also bind the blade.

• CHECK THE ELECTRICAL CORD to be sure it can follow the saw to the end of the cut without encountering the blade or catching on the end of the sheet you are cutting. Some woodworkers drape the cord over their shoulders to prevent this.

• ADJUST THE BLADE so it extends no more than $1/4$ inch deeper than the thickness of the stock. When you make the cut, position the blade on the waste side of the wood. After you finish the cut, wait for the blade to stop rotating before you set down the saw.

There are two kinds of portable circular saws: worm-drive saws have the motor parallel to the blade; sidewinder saws (above) have the motor perpendicular to the blade. Worm-drive saws are more powerful and give you a clearer look at the line you are cutting, while sidewinders weigh less and have a more stable base.

To cut a long sheet of plywood lengthwise, support with four or five 2 × 4s set across two sawhorses. Place one 2 × 4 under each side of the line where you will cut, and then use the others to support the rest of the panel. Guide the saw with a straightedge, as shown on pages 156–157.

Making a straightedge jig

Although you can buy a ready-made straightedge to guide a circular saw, a homemade one can be customized to the exact offset needed for your saw's base. The widths of saw bases vary, so factory-made straightedges don't have built-in offsets.

1 **CUT A GUIDE STRIP.** Choose a sheet of plywood that has at least one unblemished, factory-fresh edge. With a carpenter's chalk line, mark a 3-inch-wide strip that includes that edge. Cut along the line. You can do this freehand or clamp on a straight board as a guide. The cut doesn't have to be perfectly straight, as the factory edge will be your actual straightedge.

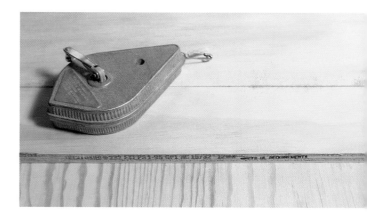

2 **ATTACH THE GUIDE STRIP.** Snap a second line for a second strip that's about as wide as the saw's base, or a little less. Place the 3-inch strip from Step 1 on the far side of the line, with the factory edge facing it. Screw the strip in place.

3 **TRIM THE EDGE.** Guiding the saw's base plate against the factory edge, trim the plywood. This automatically trims the base of the jig to reproduce the exact offset between the edge of the saw's base plate and the blade.

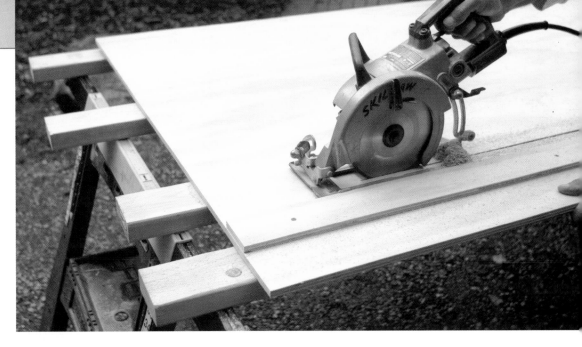

4 SEPARATE THE JIG. Cut the completed straightedge assembly from the sheet of plywood. For this cut, guide the saw against the back edge (not the factory edge) of the straightedge. Note how the side with the factory edge is wider.

5 USE IT. To use the straightedge, clamp it to the piece of wood you want to use, not over the waste section. Align the guide so that the cut you made in Step 3 just touches the line you want to cut. Keep the saw's base against the factory edge as you make the cut.

6 ABOUT CROSSCUTS. When cutting a long sheet of plywood crosswise, set it on 2 × 4s as if you were planning a lengthwise cut. Adjust the blade to cut about $\frac{1}{8}$ inch deeper than the panel is thick. Clamp down a straightedge and make the cut. The blade will nick the 2 × 4s but you can reuse them numerous times and eventually recycle them into projects where a blemished surface doesn't matter.

PRO TIP

To prevent splinters as you cut across wood fibers with a circular saw or a jigsaw, score the line with a sharp utility knife before making the cut. This precaution is necessary only on crosswise cuts, not those in line with the grain.

Some table saws are lightweight enough to carry or roll around easily. This is a heavyweight, but it's still easy to move because it's on a base with lockable casters. If you buy a table saw, check the power requirements. Lightweight saws usually run on standard 120-volt circuits, while more powerful models may require 240-volt circuits.

About table saws

While you can accomplish a lot with just a jigsaw or a circular saw, a table saw speeds up the work and helps you produce professional-looking results. For example, instead of measuring and setting up a straightedge for each cut, you can adjust the saw's fence or jig and then run all the parts through the blade, without measuring for each one.

A table saw is perfect for ripping lengthwise cuts, and it's also good for crosscuts, especially on wide material like plywood. Because a table saw produces accurate cuts, it is the best tool for making multiple cabinet parts of the same size. If you add a dado set (below, left), the saw also cuts grooves, rabbets, dadoes, and tenons. Table saws come with a rip fence to keep stock parallel to the blade and a miter gauge for perpendicular or angle cuts.

Using a table saw safely

A table saw is a powerful woodworking tool, so you must know what you are doing. Clearly, you shouldn't put your fingers in front of the blade, and you should never operate the saw without first putting on safety glasses, ear protection, and, in some cases, a mask. Other safety issues aren't so obvious. The blade rotates toward you as it cuts, which means it presses the wood against the table to produce a clean cut. This also means the back portion of the blade is rotating upward. If wood passing on either side of the spinning blade binds, the piece is likely to shoot up and back toward you at lightning speed. Most of the following safety rules are designed to prevent this.

- GUIDE THE STOCK against the rip fence or hold it tight against the miter gauge, never both.
- NEVER CUT FREEHAND. Some cuts require special jigs (such as a featherboard, page 160) to keep your hands away from the blade and to keep the wood from binding.
- STAND TO THE SIDE, not behind the blade, when you operate the saw. If you are using the rip fence, you and it usually should be on opposite sides of the blade. If you are using the miter gauge, position yourself so you are on one side of the gauge and the blade is on the other.
- ON CROSSCUTS, increase safety and accuracy by replacing the miter gauge with a crosscut sled (see photo at top of page 159). Avoid crosscutting long boards. Use a hand saw, a jigsaw, or a circular saw instead.
- ON RIP CUTS, hold on to the piece between the blade and the fence until it clears the blade. If the piece is narrow, use a push stick, not your hand. Let the cut piece on the other side of the blade fall away naturally. Do not press it

against the blade as you complete the cut, or it could kick back. A spreader, a thin metal tooth that fits behind the blade, helps guard against kickback.

• IF A BOARD IS BOWED, do not attempt to rip a straight edge on it. Instead, screw a straight-edge to it and guide that against the rip fence.

• ON NARROW CUTS, replace the standard throat plate with a zero-clearance insert, which eliminates the usual gap alongside the blade. A wide opening could allow the strip you are cutting to drop down and catch against the blade.

• AVOID WEARING GLOVES or loose sleeves that could become caught and draw your hand into the blade. If you have long hair, tie it back.

A crosscut sled consists of front and back uprights attached to a base, which in turn is attached to hardwood runners that slide in the table saw's miter gauge slots. Once you run the sled through the saw the first time, the kerf, or opening cut by the blade, shows precisely where to align stock for subsequent cuts. For accurate cuts, the fence closest to you must be perfectly perpendicular to the blade.

RIGHT: If the blade will be very close to the rip fence, attach an auxiliary wooden fence to the metal one with clamps, screws, or double-stick tape. This rabbet cut is being made with a dado blade.

LEFT: To make an angle cut on a table saw, set the miter gauge to the desired angle, grip the stock firmly, and press it against the gauge as you make the cut. Use two hands except when you're switching the saw on and off. Grip the wood and gauge until the stock completely clears the blade. Do not move the cut-off piece (waste) until the blade stops. For added safety and accuracy, create a larger bearing surface on the miter gauge by screwing a piece of wood to its front, as was done here. This cut is a compound miter, meaning that it's both an angle cut and a bevel.

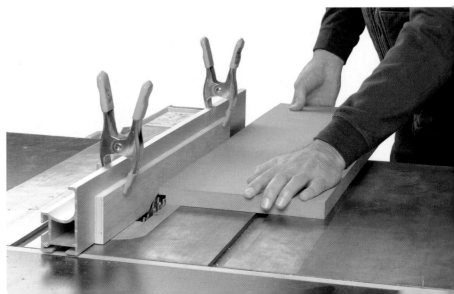

If you want to cut short pieces that are equally long, you might be tempted to use the rip fence as a measuring device while you guide the boards with the miter gauge. But that could trap wood between the blade and the fence and lead to a kickback. Instead, clamp a short block to the fence and align your cuts to that, then use the miter gauge to guide your board. There must be enough room for the stock to completely clear the block before it reaches the blade. You can use the same system if you want to make dado cuts in the same place across several boards.

What's a Featherboard?

When you are making rip cuts in thin stock, keep the piece firmly pressed against the rip fence with a featherboard—a guide piece with a series of cuts that resemble the vanes of a feather. Besides helping to ensure a straight cut, a featherboard helps prevent kickback. You can buy one or make your own from a piece of ¾-inch-thick plywood or straight-grained wood that's about 18 inches long by 5 inches wide. Cut one end at a 40-degree angle, then draw a line at the same angle about 4 inches in from the end. Using a table saw's rip fence as a guide, make a series of cuts up to the line so that you leave wooden fingers about ¼ inch wide, separated by gaps about ⅛ inch wide.

MAKING A FEATHERBOARD

Keep the long edge against the fence as you cut the fingers in a featherboard. Putting the short side there wouldn't be as safe.

USING A FEATHERBOARD

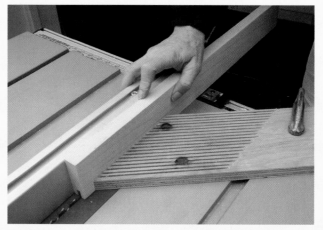

To use the featherboard, clamp it to the table so the tips press against the stock but still allow you to move the board forward without forcing it. If you are cutting through the stock, the featherboard must be completely in front of the blade. If you are cutting a groove, as shown here, the feathers can apply pressure where the blade begins to cut, but they cannot touch the stock beyond the first half of the blade, or there could be kickback.

Using power sanders

Power sanders make short work of tasks such as smoothing visible surfaces or removing bulges that keep pieces of your built-in from fitting together precisely. Because they do the job efficiently, they are an essential tool on large projects that require lots of sanding.

• A **BELT SANDER** abrades wood quickly—sometimes too quickly. It's the best tool for rough-leveling a large area, such as several boards you have glued together to make a countertop. The belt moves in only one direction, so keep the sander in constant motion or it will dig a rut in your work. You can also use a belt sander to shape a piece that you have scribed, or marked, to follow the contour of an uneven surface. Belt sanders are powerful. Tie back long hair and roll up loose sleeves so they don't get pulled into the rollers.

• A **RANDOM-ORBIT SANDER** produces a very smooth surface and can remove excess material fairly rapidly. Models with a hook-and-loop sandpaper-attachment system give you the option of switching to a different grit and still reusing the first sheet later. Other models use peel-and-stick sandpaper sheets, which cost less.

• A **PALM SANDER** produces a smooth surface but doesn't remove wood quickly. It's an ideal tool for finish sanding. It's also the safest type of power sander for children to use. Many palm sanders use a quarter sheet of standard sandpaper, which you can find at any hardware store or lumberyard.

SAFETY TIP

To keep a loose board from scooting around as you sand, set it on a piece of nonskid carpet padding.

Specialized power tools

The right power tools can speed your work, improve your results, and allow you to tackle more complicated joinery. You don't need to invest in a whole suite of tools at once. Consider renting or borrowing a tool the first time you need it so you understand its features. Then, when you are ready to buy, you'll be better equipped to shop for the features you value. While you might not need the most expensive model, the cheapest one is usually not a good deal either. It may lack power or have flimsy adjustment knobs. Good tools can last a lifetime.

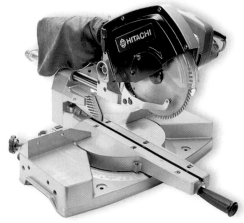

Power miter saw Often called a chop saw, a power miter saw makes crosswise cuts on narrow pieces accurately and reliably. With it, you can cut a tight-fitting face frame or make a series of shelves all the same length. You can also cut molding so that joints fit precisely. Chop saws twist on a base, allowing you to lock them at an angle (1 to 45 degrees or a little more). This is an invaluable feature if you are designing a built-in that will include molding with miter joints.

To use a chop saw safely, press the stock securely against the fence, on the left side of the blade. Ideally, you will be holding the piece you want and the waste piece will be on the right side of the blade. If you are cutting off small pieces, don't let anyone stand behind the right side of the saw, as it might shoot the cutoffs in that direction. As you complete the cut, release the trigger and raise the saw to its upright position. Continue to hold the stock until the saw shuts off. If the guard seems slow to drop into its normal position, adjust it before using the saw again.

A compound miter saw twists and pivots, allowing you to cut a piece of wood so that it has angles on both its face and edge. This feature is helpful if you are cutting a lot of wide crown molding or want to miter the ends of boards. A standard miter saw is not as sophisticated a tool, but it costs less and is fine for most built-in projects.

Planer A planer shaves boards to uniform thickness. Besides using this tool to smooth rough-cut lumber, you can also use it to create boards that are different thicknesses than those ordinarily sold at lumberyards. For example, you might want to use shelf boards that are the standard $3/4$ inch thick but plane a few boards down to $1/2$ inch for vertical dividers. Variety makes built-ins look more interesting.

Biscuit joiner Also known as a plate joiner, this tool cuts semicircular grooves that are just the right size for oval wooden biscuits. By cutting matching grooves in mating pieces, you can quickly make reinforced joints for cabinet boxes, drawers, doors, or face frames. The grooves and biscuits also help you line up surfaces, such as wooden edging with a shelf, or join boards that are being glued together to make a wider panel. If you are building with particleboard or MDF, joints held together with biscuits and glue are stronger than those made with screws and glue.

Biscuit joiners have a fence that flips up or down. To cut grooves in an edge, flip the fence down, as shown, so it rides on the top of the panel. The fence ensures that the slots are all in a straight line.

It takes little time or skill to learn to use a biscuit joiner, which probably explains its popularity. You simply move a knob to a setting that matches the size of the biscuits, adjust the fence to set the height of the grooves, and push the spring-loaded blade into the stock. After cleaning debris from the slots and testing the fit, you're ready to glue the pieces together.

To cut grooves into the side of a panel, flip the fence up and turn the tool so the fence acts as its foot. With the cord facing up and the base tight to the edge of the panel, press down on the biscuit joiner to make the cut.

To glue a biscuit joint, always test the fit and clamping system first. Apply glue to the slots but not to the biscuits. Work quickly. Glue makes wood fibers expand, so if you delay too long, the grooves can swell enough so the biscuits won't slip in easily. Clamp the joint until the glue sets.

Jointer A jointer allows you to create a flat face on a board and an edge that is at a perfect right angle to it. Owning this tool is especially important if you start with rough-cut lumber or hardwood with ragged edges. Set the rotating blades flush with the back section of the bed, then lower the front table slightly. Using blocks to keep your hands away from the blade, feed a board over the front table and onto the second. As the wood passes the knives, they will shave off a slight amount. It may take several passes to completely flatten and smooth the wood. Then tip the board on edge, with the flat side against the fence. Run the board past the knives again, until the edge is flat and at a perfect right angle to the flat face. Use a planer to flatten the other side and a table saw to cut the other edge.

JOINERY TECHNIQUES

SOME BUILT-INS ARE HELD TOGETHER with just nails or screws and maybe some glue. Others rely on traditional joinery such as dovetails and dadoes, or on more recent inventions such as the thin wooden wafers known as biscuits. The best options for your project depend on your skill and equipment, as well as on the material you are using.

Precision joinery gives the built-in shelving unit in this pocket office a clean, modern look.

Joinery for solid wood

Traditional joinery is a response to the slender, tubular nature of wood fibers and the way they behave. In a log, they are oriented lengthwise. When a tree is first cut, the wood is heavy with moisture. This eventually evaporates, which causes the fibers to shrink and leaves them filled with air. The walls of the fibers, though, continue to shrink or swell—primarily in width— as their moisture fluctuates in response to humidity in the surrounding air. Joints in solid wood must accommodate this fluctuation and overcome the fact that the ends of wood fibers don't hold glue or fasteners nearly as well as their sides do.

• TONGUE-AND-GROOVE, mortise-and-tenon, and dovetail joints provide side-to-side contact for wood fibers even when the end of one board meets another board at a right angle. Dowels and biscuits accomplish the same thing.

• GROOVE JOINTS such as dadoes and rabbets work under a different principle: Wood fibers are extremely crush resistant in their lengthwise direction. In a groove joint, part of the grooved piece physically supports the other piece.

Joinery for sheet materials

The wood fibers in plywood and particleboard don't line up in a single direction, which makes the sheets more stable dimensionally, but also reduces the strength that comes from having fibers run side-to-side. As a result, tongue-and-groove, mortise-and-tenon, and dovetail joints aren't typically used for plywood, particleboard, or MDF. However, dowels and biscuits work well with sheet materials, as do dadoes and rabbets.

Nails and screws

Metal is another good way to secure joints that aren't subject to much force, such as a bookcase or perhaps drawers that operate on modern glides. But if you want drawers on wooden runners, you need a stronger connection, such as dovetails, because these drawers tend to stick in humid weather.

Nails and screws are most likely to come loose in sheet materials. Use particleboard screws, which are thicker than ordinary ones, if you can find them. Knock-down fasteners work even better because they use bolts and nuts to create sturdy metal-to-metal connections.

Basic Joints

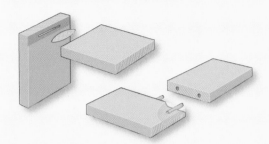

Butt joint. This is by far the easiest joint to create. An edge butt joint usually needs just glue, provided both edges are square, smooth, and flat. For a butt joint where the end of one piece fits against the edge or face of another, strengthen the connection with nails, screws, dowels, or biscuits.

Miter joint. The typical miter joint consists of two pieces of molding cut at a 45-degree angle and joined to make a 90-degree bend. Though the concept is simple, a miter joint is often tricky to get just right. A power miter saw is the best tool to make miter joints.

Dado joint. This joint consists of a groove cut into the face of a piece of wood. The mating piece slides in, creating a rigid connection between a drawer back and side, or a shelf and side of a cabinet box. Cut a dado with a router and a straight bit, or use a table saw. A dado should be no more than a quarter to a third as deep as the material is thick.

Rabbet joint. A groove cut along an edge of a piece creates this joint. It's stronger than an unreinforced butt joint. A rabbet is perfect for the rear of a cabinet box because the joint hides the end grain of the back piece.

Rabbet-and-dado joint. Use this when you need extra rigidity. Rabbet-and-dado joints are particularly effective on plywood cabinets and drawers.

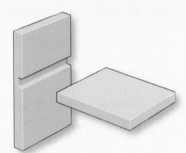

Mortise-and-tenon joint. Suitable for solid wood only, true mortise-and-tenon joints are very strong but relatively difficult to create. First create a round or oval recess with a drill press or a plunge router, then square up the edges with a chisel. Use a handsaw or power saw to cut the tenon.

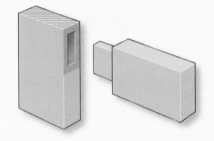

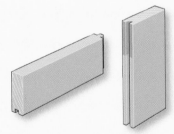

Tongue-and-groove joint. This is similar to a mortise-and-tenon joint, but it is easier to make because it extends to the ends of pieces. Use both a router and a straight bit, a rail-and-stile set in a router table, or a table saw (see pages 154 and 158).

Dovetail joint. Strong and decorative, dovetails are the traditional way to join drawer sides and other box-like structures. Though you can make them with a handsaw and a chisel, they're easier done with a router, a dovetail bit, and a dovetail jig.

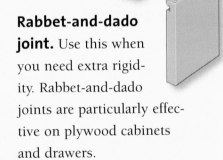

SIZING UP YOUR SPACE

WITH BUILT-INS, MEASURING CAN GET COMPLICATED, especially if you are designing a project that will span an entire wall or that needs to fit precisely between other fixed elements, such as windows or doors. If you're off by ⅛ inch on one measurement, then ⅛ inch on another, and another after that, you could wind up with a built-in that doesn't fit.

The steps below can help ensure accuracy. Using a computer or a pencil and paper, sketch the room and note your measurements on the drawing. Depending on how elaborate your project is, you might want to create one sketch for the floor and separate sketches for each wall.

1 **ESTABLISH A REFERENCE POINT.** Use a carpenter's level (above) to determine whether your starting point, such as a wall or a piece of door trim, is plumb. If the surface slants, make a vertical mark that is plumb and measure up at a convenient distance. Make a cross mark over the vertical line there and use that as your reference point for subsequent measurements.

2 **TAKE THE FIRST MEASUREMENT.** From the reference point, measure over to the next significant feature, such as the outside edge of the trim around a window. Note this dimension on a piece of paper as you begin to create a sketch of the wall.

3 **FIND THE NEXT POINT.** Measure over from the initial starting point to the next significant feature. Here, that's the far side of the window molding. Use the same starting point each time you measure along a wall so you don't compound errors. If you were to measure the first distance and then went from there for the second measurement and were ⅛ inch too short each time, you would be ¼ inch behind as you started the third measurement.

4 **CREATE A CORNER.** If your built-in will extend around a corner where there is a gap, such as for a bay window, determine where an extension of the next wall would meet the first wall. Tack a string to the far end of the second wall and pull it taut. With the string barely touching the wall, mark where it butts into the first wall. Then replace the string with a board in the same location. (If the two walls already meet at a corner, skip this step.)

5 **FIND THE ANGLE.** From the intersecting corner, or, in this case, the point where the corners would meet, mark back 4 feet along one wall and 3 feet in the other direction. Check whether the two marks are 5 feet apart. If so, the corner is square and you can proceed to measure the second wall as you did the first. If not, move the board or mark the floor to show where the second wall would need to be to create a right angle. Base the second wall's measurements on that line.

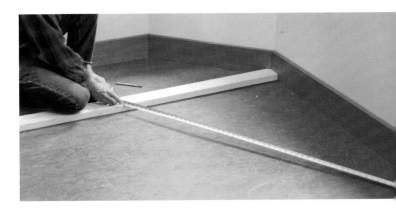

Using a Story Pole

Instead of measuring a space with a tape and then jotting down all those little fractions of an inch on a sheet of paper, you can mark your measurements on a piece of wood and use it as a guide. Known as a story pole, the marked piece is a handy reference as you design and build. Story poles are particularly useful for built-ins that will have multiple components. This vanity, for example, consists of five cabinet boxes, including the narrow one with drawers in the middle.

To lay out a vanity like the one shown here, you'll need two pieces of wood that together span the width of the room and overlap a bit (a single piece would be unwieldly). After noting the overlap, mark off at least 1 inch at each end for a filler strip along the wall. This is the minimum swing space needed for a full-overlay door. Then divide up the remaining space by the number of cabinets you want. Mark the thickness of each cabinet side plus $1/2$-inch-wide spaces for drawer glides ("GLD" on the story pole at right). That leaves you with the remaining drawer ("DRW") dimensions. You could make another story pole, showing vertical dimensions to define drawer heights.

A story pole not only helps you visualize how much space you are devoting to each component, but it also makes it less likely that you will forget to leave space for something important. For example, if you were just tallying measurements, you might overlook the fact that you must allow for two thicknesses of cabinet material where cabinet boxes meet. With two big X's holding the space on a story pole, you're less likely to make this mistake.

ABOUT SHELVES

SHELVES ARE PROBABLY THE SIMPLEST TYPE OF BUILT-IN. Options range from basic shelves fitted into a niche to elaborate bookcases trimmed with molding. Because built-in shelves are designed for the space where they are installed, they can use every available inch.

• THE MAXIMUM HEIGHT for a top shelf is 72 inches if you want most adults to reach it comfortably without using a stepladder. Leave at least a foot between the highest shelf and the top of your bookcase or other limiting enclosure, such as a ceiling.

• THE DEPTH of shelves depends on what you will store and where you will build. Above a kitchen countertop, shelves are usually 12 inches deep. Under counter-tops, they can be up to 24 inches deep to take advantage of the extra space.

• THE THICKNESS of the shelves themselves depends on the material and its ability to resist sagging. The chart below shows the maximum distance that will keep shelves from sagging more than $1/8$ inch over 45 inches. It assumes that items on the shelves weigh up to 40 pounds per square foot, a heavy load.

Floating shelves have no visible means of support. Instead, they are suspended on rods that fit into studs.

Choosing edging

Although plywood and particleboard make good shelves, most people don't want to see the ragged edges of these materials in finished projects. Edging covers the evidence. There are two basic types: iron-on and solid wood.

RECOMMENDED SPAN BETWEEN SUPPORTS

OAK OR MAPLE			
Thickness	$3/4$"	1"	$1^3/4$"
Span	36"	49"	85"

PLYWOOD			
Thickness	$5/8$"	$3/4$"	1"
Span	29"	34"	46"

CHERRY OR POPLAR			
Thickness	$3/4$"	1"	$1^3/4$"
Span	34"	45"	79"

SOFT PINE			
Thickness	$3/4$"	1"	$1^3/4$"
Span	33"	44"	76"

MDF			
Thickness	$5/8$"	$3/4$"	1"
Span	18"	21"	28"

PARTICLE-BOARD			
Thickness	$5/8$"	$3/4$"	1"
Span	16"	19"	25"

Iron-on edging This is a thin strip of wood or plastic with heat-activated adhesive on the back.

1 **IRON EDGING.** Heat an iron as specified by the edging manufacturer. Leave the water reservoir empty. While the iron heats, cut oversize lengths of the edging with scissors or a utility knife. Press straight down with the iron to activate the adhesive. Pick up the iron, move it to the next section, and press down again.

2 **ROLL EDGING.** With a roller designed for applying laminate, immediately put pressure on the edging to secure it to the board.

3 **TRIM THE ENDS.** Use a sharp utility knife and a square to neatly cut excess edging from the corners.

4 **TRIM THE EDGES.** To trim excess width from edging, hold the blade of a utility knife flat against the shelf as you pull the knife toward you. If you have a lot of edging to apply, purchase an edging trimmer, an inexpensive tool that's almost foolproof to use.

Solid wood edging Screen molding, which is sold in flat and beaded styles, makes good edging for ¾-inch-thick sheet material.

1 **CUT AND GLUE.** Place the shelf upside down on a flat work surface. Cut the edging to length. Apply glue sparingly to the back of the edging and press it against the shelf edge. Press down on the edging to align it with the surface that will be the shelf's top.

2 **TACK THE MOLDING IN PLACE.** Use wire nails, which are thin and have small heads, to hold the molding to the shelf. Set the nails with a nail set and fill the holes later with wood filler, if you wish.

BRACKET SHELVES

BRACKET SHELVES ARE SIMPLE TO BUILD and are adaptable to a wide range of styles. You can build and install a single shelf as a bookshelf in a home office, or gang several together to create the look of a built-in wall system for a living room. By widening the shelf, you can use the same basic design to make a night-stand by a bed or a table in an entryway. Or add a rod and make a bathroom built-in where you can hang a damp towel below and stack a pile of fresh towels above. If you beef up the supports, a thick bracket shelf can become a bench in a mudroom or in an entryway.

BELOW: Bracket shelves have been used for centuries because they are easy to build with simple tools. Their traditional look goes well with the relaxed country look of this pantry.

ABOVE: Three bracket shelves were all it took to create this efficient mudroom. The top two shelves have hooks for jackets, while the bottom shelf provides two-layer storage for shoes.

Doing it yourself versus buying

It's possible to buy a pair of brackets, hang them on a wall, and set a shelf on top. But building your own brackets can result in a stronger shelf and a look that's more design-forward than most of the bracket products sold in stores. One of the main advantages of building brackets yourself is that you can create a design to fit your décor.

Bracket designs Brackets are basically right triangles, with the top and back square to each other. However, the angled side, which faces out, needn't be straight, as seen in most of the ones shown below. For design inspiration, look at crown molding, as its cross section almost always makes a pleasing bracket shape. Or wander a neighborhood filled with houses from Victorian or Craftsman periods. They often feature roof brackets or other elements that you can adapt. For maximum strength, design your brackets so that they are taller than wide (or at least equal in the case of the quarter-circle at far right).

Whatever style you choose, sketch your design on paper or cardboard to make a template. Cut the template to size and use it to trace your design onto the wood you will use for your brackets.

A pair of bracket shelves creates useful display and storage space and keeps clutter off the floor of this small living room. A bracket shelf by a window is a great place to grow plants.

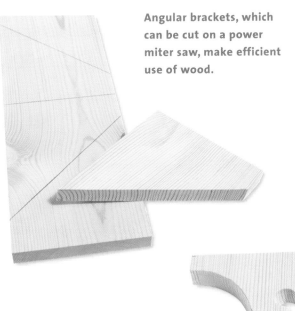

Angular brackets, which can be cut on a power miter saw, make efficient use of wood.

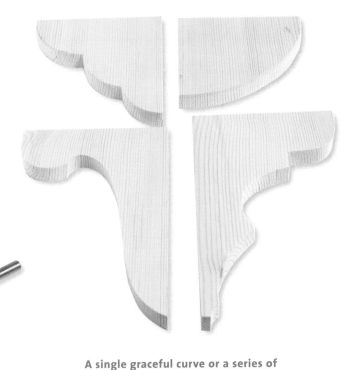

Cutouts in the bracket itself are easy to make with a Forstner bit.

A single graceful curve or a series of them makes a handsome bracket.

Building a bracket shelf

To determine the appropriate spacing between brackets for the type of shelf material you're using, see page 168. The shelves can be a few inches wider than the brackets, and the ends can cantilever a short distance as well. Brackets ¾ inch thick work well in most cases, unless you are building a bench or a shelf that will support large potted plants or other heavy items. In that case, use material 1½ inches thick.

Adding a brace at the back strengthens the shelf and makes it easier to install, particularly if the shelf is long and has three or more brackets. The brace automatically lines up the brackets and makes it easier to fasten the unit to studs, since they don't need to line up with the brackets.

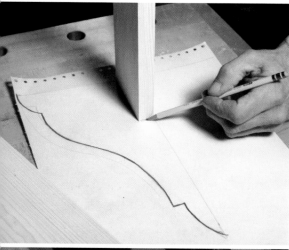

1 **DESIGN A BRACE.** Once you have made a template of your bracket, incorporate a brace into its design. A brace, which supports the back of the shelf where it meets the wall, can run between brackets if there are just two. If your shelf requires more brackets, or if you want to extend the brace so that it supports the entire length of a shelf that cantilevers beyond the end brackets, you will need to notch the back of the brackets to accommodate the thickness and depth of the brace. Add this detail, if desired, to your bracket template.

2 **CUT THE BRACKETS.** Using the template, trace the shape on solid wood, plywood, or MDF. Although you can cut curves with either a narrow compass saw or a D-shaped coping saw, it's much easier to cut brackets with a jigsaw fitted with a narrow blade designed for curves. A band saw or a scroll saw also works well. Cut just to the outside of the line so that you can still see it.

3 **SMOOTH THE EDGES.** With a rasp or sandpaper, smooth the outside (cut) edge of each bracket.

If you use a rasp, pull it toward the center of your work, as making a back-and-forth motion can chip fibers on the outer edges of the brackets. Because the brackets won't be right next to each other, you won't notice slight variations in their shape, so don't fret if they are not precise copies of each other. If you have cut brackets out of plywood, plug gaps in the outside edge with wood filler, allow it to dry, then sand again.

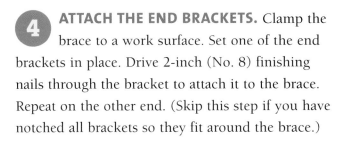

4 **ATTACH THE END BRACKETS.** Clamp the brace to a work surface. Set one of the end brackets in place. Drive 2-inch (No. 8) finishing nails through the bracket to attach it to the brace. Repeat on the other end. (Skip this step if you have notched all brackets so they fit around the brace.)

5 **ATTACH THE BRACE.** Set the brace upside down on a flat work surface. Set in place any brackets you have notched. Screw through the brace into each of the notched brackets. Use a square to make sure the bracket is straight.

6 **ADD THE SHELF AND FINISH.** Place the brace with its back facing down, then clamp spacers to your work surface to keep the brace from scooting away from you as you attach the shelf with nails or screws. If you want a smooth surface on the shelf, countersink the heads and cover them with wood filler or wooden plugs cut flush. Apply the finish of your choice, which could include paint, stain, or varnish.

7 **INSTALL THE SHELF.** With a carpenter's level and a pencil, mark the wall to show the bottom edge of the brace. Use a stud finder or tap on the wall to locate studs, then mark them, perhaps with low-tack painter's tape. Attach the shelf by screwing through the brace into studs. If the shelf will hold only a light load, you could instead attach keyhole hangers to the back and slip them over screws secured either to studs or to drywall hangers designed to carry the appropriate weight.

ALCOVE SHELVES

ALCOVE SHELVES FIT INTO NOOKS and other spaces that are walled in on three sides. They are another example of a simple built-in that can be used in a number of ways. For example, you can add a shelf or series of shelves to a closet, create a work surface, or even make a bench.

Alcove shelves are typically supported by boards known as ledger strips, which are nailed or screwed to studs within the wall. In most cases, you can make ledger strips out of wood stock as skinny as $^3/_4$ inch thick by $1^1/_2$ inches wide. Ledger strips that support a closet rod or hooks, in addition to a shelf, should be at least $3^1/_2$ inches wide. For especially heavy-duty situations, such as benches, use 2 × 4s. On the other hand, if the shelves will be made of glass or will carry only light-weight decorative items, quarter-round molding might be more attractive.

Alcove shelves have such a simple design that the construction steps might seem obvious. However, getting the shelf to fit precisely is a bit tricky, especially if the sidewalls of the alcove are not parallel.

Built like an alcove shelf, a bench fits what was originally a narrow coat closet. Eliminating the closet doors and recessing the bench made the entry seem more spacious.

Practical and easy to make, alcove shelves add display space to the end of a hallway.

1 **INSTALL LEDGER STRIPS.** Use a level and a pencil to mark the bottom of the ledger strips. Run a stud sensor across the walls or tap on them to locate the studs. Cut one ledger strip that spans the back of the alcove and two that fit the shelf width or a little less, minus the thickness of the back ledger. Screw the back ledger to the wall into the studs. Attach the side ledgers in the same way. If there aren't enough studs to attach each strip in at least two places, use toggle bolts or other drywall anchors.

2 **ROUGH-CUT THE SHELF AND FIT ONE END.** Measure the width of the opening at several places and cut the shelf board $1\frac{1}{4}$ to 2 inches longer than the longest dimension. Put the board in place against the back wall, but tip up one end. Adjust a scribing tool (the kind of inexpensive compass used to draw circles) to the biggest gap along the edge that's slanting down, or about $\frac{1}{2}$ inch if the gap is narrow. Hold the scriber upright, with the tip against the wall, and trace the angle of the wall onto the board.

3 **CUT THE LINE.** Depending on how much material you need to remove, use a jigsaw or a belt sander to trim the shelf to the scribed line. Make a square cut at the front of the shelf, but gradually tip the saw or sander toward the outside of the line so the edge slants slightly inward as you cut toward the back. This makes it easier to trim off a little more material later, if necessary.

4 **MARK LENGTHS AND SCRIBE AGAIN.** Measure the width of the alcove at the back and where the front of the shelf will be. Measuring from the end you just trimmed, mark these two dimensions on the top of the shelf board. Put the shelf back on the ledgers, with the untrimmed end slanted down and the back of the shelf flush against the back wall. Set the scriber to the distance between one of the marks and the wall. Scribe the line. It should pass over the other mark. Trim the excess length from the shelf, as in Step 3. Set the shelf in place. If it doesn't rest flat on the ledgers, trim or sand as needed. If you see gaps between the shelf and the back wall, scribe and trim the back edge as well.

WHEN TO USE TEMPLATES

Tilting and scribing is only one way to create a shelf or countertop that fits precisely in a space. If you are dealing with a non-rectangular shape, you'll probably want to make a template and then build the part to match. See pages 176, 183, and 185 for several ways to make templates. The best option for each situation depends on the complexity of the shape and the template materials you have on hand.

A SHELF-TYPE WINDOW SEAT

THERE ARE TWO BASIC WAYS TO BUILD A WINDOW SEAT or a bench: as a low cabinet or as an enhanced shelf. The cabinet approach works best when you are starting with an open wall, but if you have an existing alcove, such as the space around a bay window or the niche created by a dormer window, a shelf-style seat is easier to build and will generally cost less. The basic construction steps are roughly the same as if you were adding a shelf to an alcove. With a few more steps, you can give your window seat a more finished appearance by enclosing the base. That not only looks better but also gives you the option of creating a hidden storage space under the seat.

1 **DETERMINE THE ANGLE.** Place a straightedge across the opening of the alcove or along a line that is at a right angle to an adjoining wall, as shown in Step 5 on page 166. Then use an adjustable bevel gauge to make a rough template to determine the angle.

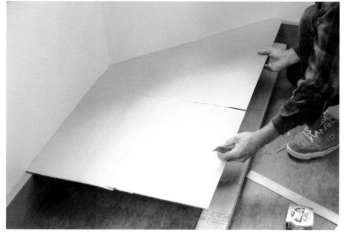

2 **FLIP THE TEMPLATE.** If the angles in the alcove are the same, as they are in this example and with most bay windows, flip the rough template you made in Step 1. Copy the template to create one for the window seat's other angled corner. Keep the templates oversized along their front edges for now.

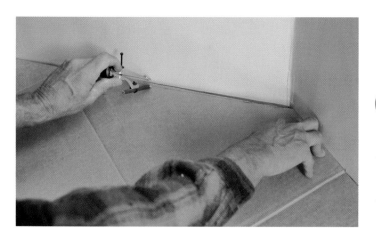

3 **SCRIBE AND TRIM.** If you see gaps between the rough template and the wall, fine-tune the template one edge at a time. Set a scriber to the widest gap and trace its shape on the cardboard. Then trim the cardboard to fit. Repeat for the other wall if necessary. Then make additional templates for the remaining space. Tape the parts together.

4 **ESTABLISH A LINE.** Draw a level line showing the top of the ledger strips that will support the back of the window seat. Window seats are generally most comfortable if they're about 18 inches high, so determine the ledger height by subtracting the thickness of whatever cushions you will use and the bench seat itself.

5 **INSTALL LEDGERS.** To create a solid base for the seat, cut a frame of 2 × 4s for the back, sides, and front. Use the template to help you determine lengths and angles. Screw the back and sides to the wall along the level line you drew, then attach the front. At each stud, use two screws at least 3½ inches long. Use a level to make sure the frame doesn't slope.

6 **ADD CROSS BRACES.** Add a couple of 2 × 4 braces between the front and back of the seat. If you want storage underneath, place the braces where they will support the sides of a lift-up door. On a bay window, the best places for cross braces are from each back corner to the front. Cut a notch ¾ inch wide and 1 inch deep on the bottom front of each brace so you can slip in the front panel, as described in Step 15 on page 179. Attach the braces by driving screws through the front framing and at an angle into the back ledger.

7 **TRIM THE FRONT EDGE.** Set the template pieces on the ledgers and mark the front edge where it is flush with the outside face of the framing. Cut the cardboard along that line, then check the fit one more time.

8 **TRANSFER THE SHAPE AND CUT.** Place the template on the bench material. For this window seat, the homeowner chose ¾-inch-thick maple plywood. Tape down the cardboard so it doesn't shift. Using a pencil, trace the edges onto the plywood. Clamp a straightedge over the seat shape, score along the cut line with a utility knife, then cut off the excess plywood with a circular saw or a jigsaw.

continued ▶▶

9 **MARK THE BRACES.** Place the cut seat on the framing. At the front and back, mark where the center of each brace lies underneath the bench material.

10 **DEFINE THE DOOR.** Between the centerlines you established in Step 9, draw a line about 3 inches in from the back edge. Draw perpendicular lines along the centerlines of the braces from the back line you have just drawn to the front of the seat. Score these lines with a utility knife.

11 **CUT THE DOOR.** Clamp a straightedge along the line for the back of the door. To begin cutting at the start of the line, you'll need to make a plunge cut. A few inches forward of the start of the line, place the saw at an angle so that the front of its base touches the straightedge but the blade doesn't. Retract the blade guard with one hand, and switch on the saw with the other. Carefully lower the spinning blade into the wood and cut forward. Before you reach the end of the door line, switch off the saw. When the blade stops, lift and reposition the saw, and cut the sides. Finish the corner cuts with a jigsaw or a handsaw.

12 **MAKE THE BACK LIP.** Now place the cut seat back on the frame. Make a lip to support the back of the lid by fitting a length of 2-by-³/₄-inch wood or plywood between the cross braces. Position it under the seat and press it back against the back ledger. Clamp it to the seat. Then remove the seat, turn it over, and screw on the lip.

13 **ATTACH A HINGE.** With a hacksaw, cut a piano hinge so it's slightly shorter than the lid is wide. Screw it to the seat and the lid.

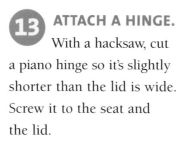

14 **ADD THE FRONT.** Cut the front panel so it spans the width of the seat at the front (or cut two panels and design a decorative detail to hide the seam where they meet at the center). The height should allow the panel to fit behind the front framing in the notches you cut into the cross braces in Step 6 on page 177. Screw the front panel to the framing from the back.

15 **ATTACH THE TOP.** Slide the seat into place and fasten it by driving a few nails or screws into the ledgers and framing.

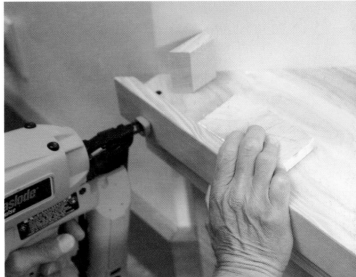

16 **ADD A FRONT LIP.** To keep cushions from sliding off, and to cover the bench's plywood edge, nail to the front a strip of wood about 3 inches wide by ³/₄ inch thick. Elevate the strip by ³/₄ inch or so. Miter the ends to fit against the wall, or plug gaps there with mitered stubs cut from the same material. Also nail baseboard or other molding along the bottom edge.

17 **ADD A DOOR OPENER.** The final step gives you a way to open the door to the storage area. Install a recessed ring pull near the center front, or drill a hole about ⁷/₈ inch wide, big enough to slip a finger through. If you drill, clamp a scrap block underneath to prevent splinters, and use a clean-cutting Forstner bit.

ADJUSTABLE SHELVES

ADJUSTABLE SHELVES ARE MORE POPULAR than fixed ones, even among people who rarely, if ever, change the spacing. Besides the obvious benefit of providing more options for storing different objects of varying heights, movable shelves are easy to repaint if you decide to change your décor. The support systems for adjustable shelves vary.

Tracks and brackets

Metal sleeve

Shelf pin

Shelf pins

• **TRACKS AND BRACKETS** allow you to hang shelves directly on a wall. Some systems include a hanging rail at the top, which you screw to studs. Then you just hook the vertical standards to the rail, eliminating the need to line up each one individually. Weight limits vary considerably, so check before you purchase a system. In some cases, shelves can carry a heavier load if you fasten the uprights to the wall, after first hanging them from the top rail. Because the tracks go on the surface of the wall, shelves wind up with a gap at the back. You can plug the gaps by nailing thin strips of wood to the backs of the shelves between uprights. Some uprights have a single line of slots for the brackets, while sturdier systems have pairs of slots.

• **HOLE-AND-PIN SYSTEMS** are the easiest and most popular way to create adjustable shelves when the shelves fit between uprights made of solid wood, plywood, particleboard, or MDF. (Drywall is not strong enough to support pins.) Be careful to match the shelf pins' diameter to the size of the holes. Some support pins are a metric size (often 5 millimeters), while others are standard (often $\frac{1}{4}$ inch).

• **TRACK-AND-CLIP SYSTEMS** can be used to support shelves within cabinets, bookcases, or similar spaces. Slots in the tracks are closer together than holes for pins, so you get more leeway in adjusting shelves. Although it's possible to nail tracks to cabinet sides, recessed standards, which fit in a groove, create a more finished look and eliminate gaps at the ends of shelves.

• **WOODEN STANDARDS,** often found in kitchen cabinets from the early 1900s, are a nice touch for built-ins where there is a face frame to tuck the strips behind. Nail, screw, or glue the notched uprights into place and move the horizontal supports to adjust the shelves.

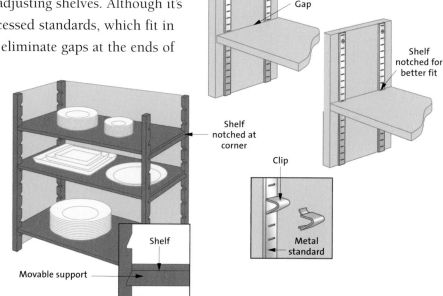

Surface-mounted tracks

Gap

Shelf notched for better fit

Shelf notched at corner

Clip

Metal standard

Shelf

Movable support

The Floating-Shelf Look

Although track-and-bracket systems are often relegated to garages and utility rooms, you can dress them up enough to mimic a more elaborate built-in. First, buy or paint the standards to match the wall. Then hide the brackets by nailing or gluing 3-inch-by-$^3/_4$-inch wooden strips along exposed, room-facing edges of the shelves. Make sure the top of each strip is flush with the top of the shelf.

The upper levels of these faux floating shelves are made of pine boards, each about 1 inch thick. The bottom shelf, which spans a greater length, is made of 1-inch-thick oak. It has an extra right-angle wall bracket at its far end so it can be used as a bench.

LEFT: Pins are used to support the glass shelves in this display niche. To keep the area from looking like the inside of a prefab cabinet, there are no rows of empty holes, just the ones that are in use. Drilling only the holes you need is one option when you create built-ins with this kind of shelf-support system. You can always add additional holes later should you need them.

RIGHT: Nailing tracks to the sides of a cabinet or bookcase is quick and easy, but it results in gaps at the ends of the shelves. For a tighter fit than the one shown at right, recess the tracks or notch the ends of the shelves so the tracks can pass through.

C-SHAPED PANTRY SHELVES

WHEN A CLOSET IS TOO DEEP to reach into easily yet not deep enough to be a true walk-in, C-shaped shelves are often the best alternative. They typically begin on one side of a closet, wrap across the back, and then return on the other side. In the middle, they give you a little standing room. The style has long been popular for pantry shelves, but it's suitable for other situations, including alcoves where you want to store considerable quantities but don't want to sacrifice convenience or access. C-shaped shelves don't fill the full depth of a space, meaning they don't store as much as rectangular shelves, but items are easy to see and retrieve.

The main challenges in building C-shaped shelves are working within a confined space and ensuring an accurate fit for the shelves. Although you can create a template as shown on pages 176–177, dealing with floppy sheets of cardboard is awkward in a tight space. Following are two other template methods. One system came from boatbuilders who needed a way to replicate complicated shapes in enclosed spaces. The other system was developed by cabinet installers making quick templates for countertops.

The C-shaped shelves in this pantry achieve the right balance between maximizing storage space and keeping everything accessible. The shelves are 18 inches deep along one side and 14 inches deep along the other. At the back, they are 12 inches deep.

1 **A BOATBUILDER TEMPLATE.** To the floor, tape a piece of paper that's slightly smaller than the space you intend to fill with shelves. Find a pointed piece of scrap trim of a convenient length. In several spots on each wall, and at corners or places where features such as uprights (described in Steps 8–10) will jut out from the wall, touch the point to the wall and trace around the other end of the stick. The more tracings you make, the greater your accuracy, provided you don't make so many marks that they appear to be a jumble.

2 **TRANSFER THE MARKS.** Tape the paper to template material such as inexpensive hardboard, then line up the stick with one tracing. Mark the spot where the pointed end reaches. Repeat for the other tracings.

3 **CONNECT THE DOTS.** Draw lines connecting the places you marked in Step 2. Cut out the template along the lines. You don't need to fill in the gaps between the uprights with template material, as you can take care of that later in Step 11. You now have an outline of the closet's walls, plus the width of the uprights. As your particular closet or space permits, add shelf widths to create a C shape and cut that out too. Be sure to allow for the width of the edging described in Step 7.

4 **TEST THE FIT.** Move the template into the closet so you can make sure you will be able to maneuver the shelves through its doorway. Hoist the template all the way to the top, checking the fit as you go. If you discover a bulge in the wall, note how much to trim from the back of the shelf that will be in that position. This saves a lot of work later.

5 **MARK SHELF BOARDS.** Make a simple scale drawing of a sheet of plywood and use it to determine the most efficient layout for cutting the shapes you need. Then trace the template onto the shelf material ($\frac{3}{4}$-inch-thick hardwood ply-wood was used in this project).

continued ▶▶

6 **CUT OUT THE SHELVES.** Clamp a straightedge along one line and proceed to cut out the shelves with a jigsaw or a circular saw. Where shelves angle across a corner or where a cut could mar a nearby piece, follow instructions for making a plunge cut in Step 11 on page 178. If you use a circular saw, clean up corners with a jigsaw or a handsaw.

7 **ADD EDGING.** Although it's fine to cover the front edges of the shelves with iron-on edging (see page 169), solid wood edging is more durable and helps stiffen the shelves. Use flat strips of wood ³/₄ inch thick by 1¹/₂ inches wide. Better yet, cut a groove in the back of the strip with a router or table saw. With a miter box and a fine-tooth handsaw or, preferably, with a power miter saw, cut the edging to fit. Test the fit, then glue and nail the pieces in place.

8 **MAKE UPRIGHTS.** This project requires six upright panels with tracks and clips to hold up the shelves. You'll need one panel on each wall next to the door, plus a pair of panels at each back corner. The panels don't reach all the way to the ceiling, just to the height of the tallest shelf. Their width matches the ends of the shelves. Cut the panels to fit, then use a router with an edge guide to cut a groove that matches the width and depth of the tracks.

9 **INSTALL TRACKS.** Starting at the bottom of each upright, tap the tracks into the grooves and fasten them with nails. If numbers are embossed on the tracks to help you insert clips at equal heights, make sure all of the numbers read in the same direction. If you need to cut tracks to get the height you need, use a hacksaw. If the tracks are too short for your space, add sections at the top.

10 **INSTALL UPRIGHTS.** Screw the uprights to the wall so that the fasteners you use will penetrate into the studs. If studs aren't in the appropriate places, install drywall anchors first. To do this, first set the panel in place and drill through it with a pilot bit. Move the panel aside and fasten the anchor to the spot you drilled. Then move the panel back into place and attach it.

11 **PLUG GAPS.** Before you install the shelves, decide whether you want to plug gaps between the uprights at the back of each shelf. If so, cut filler strips that match the thickness of the uprights and nail them to the backs of the shelves in the appropriate places. Because of the tight fit within the closet, you'll need to angle the filler strips' ends and install them with the long end on top so that they are easier to tilt into position.

12 **POSITION THE SHELVES.** Maneuver the shelves into the closet and stack them on the floor, or rest them on an edge of any baseboard molding.

13 **RAISE THE SHELVES INTO PLACE.** Once all of the shelves are within the alcove, lift and tilt each one in succession. Insert shelf clips underneath as your storage needs dictate.

Making a Hot-Glue Template

Many cabinet installers create countertop templates with hot glue and strips of $1/8$-inch-thick plywood, often called "door skin" because factories use it to cover doors. Strips of plywood $1/4$ inch thick would also work. Hot glue cools almost instantly, so templates go together quickly. Place a strip several inches wide along one wall. Wherever you see a gap or a change in the direction of the wall, glue on another strip to create a frame that touches all the edges. Add a diagonal brace or two to the template before you move it, just to keep it rigid.

MAKING BOOKCASES

BOOKCASES ARE BASICALLY JUST BOXES. While some simple designs consist only of a top, a bottom, sides, and shelves, there's good reason to include a back as well. Even if the back butts up to a wall and therefore might seem superfluous, it helps keep the bookcase square and sturdy. The basic construction steps for built-in bookcases are the same as for movable ones.

Choosing materials Pine 1 × 10s or 1 × 12s make serviceable shelves and are an economical choice if you want the look of solid wood with knots. If you don't want to see knots, consider using sheet material for the case and reserving solid wood for edges and trim. Hardwood plywood ³⁄₄ inch thick works well whether you opt for a clear finish or paint. If your shelf spans will be short (see the chart on page 168), MDF, particleboard, and melamine-coated particleboard also work well, but they don't give you the option of a clear finish.

For the back of a bookcase, use ¹⁄₄- or ¹⁄₂-inch-thick plywood, or thin sheets of hardboard or MDF. A thicker back adds more strength. If the back will be exposed—for example, where a bookcase doubles as a room divider—use material ¹⁄₂ to ³⁄₄ inch thick.

Sizing components If you want a large built-in bookcase 8 feet wide and 8 feet tall, save time, effort, and strain on your back by dividing it into smaller components—for example, four boxes that are each 4 feet square or eight that are 2 feet wide by 4 feet tall. If you do opt to build a tall cabinet, make sure it is not so tall that you can't tip it upright into position once it's built.

Dressing Up a Basic Bookcase

By adding a face frame or crown molding, you can give a basic bookcase a built-in look. If you want the built-in to resemble furniture, substitute a pedestal base for a 2 × 4 toe-kick base, or cover a standard toe-kick with molding shaped to look like a pedestal base. See pages 218–221 for more tips on using molding to make a bookcase look built in.

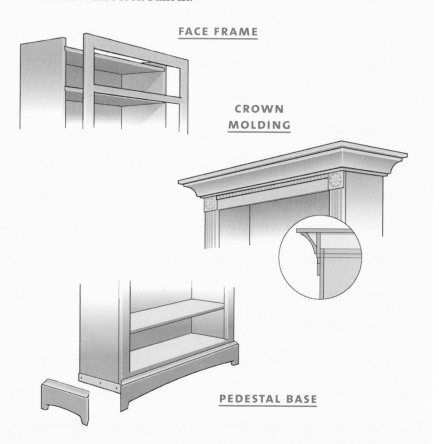

FACE FRAME

CROWN MOLDING

PEDESTAL BASE

SHELVES FIXED IN DADO JOINTS

Bookcase bases Built-in bookcases that extend to the floor generally look best if the bottom shelf is slightly elevated. Build a base of 2 × 4s or other material and set the bookcase on that. Make the base shallower than the bookcase if you want a recessed toe-kick similar to that found on most kitchen cabinets. Or, if you want a base that's a proud pedestal for the bookshelves above it, make the base the same depth as the bookcase and add baseboard molding to give it more visual weight at the bottom.

Cutting pieces If you are working with sheet material like plywood, lay out the case piece and shelves to take advantage of the sheet's size, which is typically 4 by 8 feet. Cut plywood pieces so their long dimension runs the length of the panel, as plywood is strongest in that direction.

RABBET JOINT

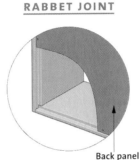

Back panel

ADJUSTABLE SHELVES

Orienting Boards

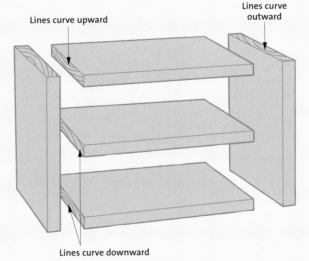

If you build a bookcase from solid wood, orient the boards to minimize problems caused by cupping. Inspect the curved lines visible on the ends. These lines tend to straighten out as the wood dries.

• FOR SHELVES, place boards so the lines curve down. Each shelf may cup on the top, but it won't form a hump at the center, which would cause things to wobble.

• FOR THE TOP, place the lines curving up. This keeps the joint with the sides tight at the front, where it's most noticeable.

• FOR THE SIDES, place the lines curving out. This also helps keep joints with the top and shelves tight.

Lines curve upward

Lines curve outward

Lines curve downward

Building a bookcase with fixed shelves

Simple to build and sturdy, a pine bookcase can rest on the floor or be hung from a wall, either alone or in combination with base cabinets. If you make several bookcases, you can combine them to outfit a pantry or office, or create a wall system for a living room or den.

The steps shown here feature a "ladder" construction, with fixed shelves in dadoes. But you could substitute butt joints fastened with nails or screws.

This bookcase is made from 1×10 pine boards ripped to $8^{1}/_{2}$ inches wide. The uprights are 48 inches tall, and the shelves are 29 inches long, making a total width for the cases of 30 inches after you allow for the two $^{1}/_{4}$-inch-deep dadoes. A 1×4 pine strip at the bottom closes in the base, and another at the top serves as a nail rail where you can attach the case to a wall.

Working with Glue

If possible, work with a helper as you are gluing the shelves in place. This reduces the chance that you'll smear glue around as you try to get the parts to line up, and it speeds assembly. Working quickly is an advantage because wood fibers swell when they absorb moisture from the glue. If this happens before you get the parts together, you may find that you need to force the shelves into the dadoes. If you are working alone, consider using white wood glue rather than yellow. Although yellow glue is slightly stronger, it sets up faster. White glue gives you more assembly time.

1 **MAKE THE UPRIGHTS.** Cut the uprights and clamp them together so they lie flat. Mark the shelf locations. Clamp a straight board across the sides to guide the router's base plate as you cut a groove for each shelf. To save you from having to calculate the offset for the router base each time, make a test cut on scrap wood and use that as a measuring device, as shown for the jigsaw guide on page 153. Make sure the guide strip is square to the edges of both boards. Put a $^{3}/_{4}$-inch-wide straight bit in a router and then cut a groove $^{1}/_{4}$ inch deep. If you have only a smaller bit, plan on making multiple passes.

2 **CUT SHELVES AND GLUE ONE SIDE.** Cut shelf boards to length. Slide them into the dadoes to make sure all the parts fit. Lightly mark the outside of the uprights to show the centerlines of the shelves. Disassemble the pieces. Spread wood glue in the dadoes on one side. Coat one end of a shelf with glue and slip the piece into its dado. Then nail through the outside of the dado into the shelf with two $1^{1}/_{2}$-inch (4d) finishing nails. Drive each nail at least 1 inch from the edge of the upright. Repeat for other shelves.

3 **ASSEMBLE THE OTHER SIDE.** Add glue to the dadoes in the other upright and to all the free ends of the shelves. Fit the shelves so they're headed into the grooves, then tap on the bookcase side to seat the shelves all the way. If the end of the bookcase will be visible, hammer against a scrap of wood so you don't mar the side. Turn the bookcase on the side you assembled first and nail the shelves in place.

4 **ADD THE BASE AND NAIL RAIL.** Cut two 1 × 4 strips to the length of the shelves, minus ½ inch to account for the ¼-inch dadoes. Place one strip at the bottom, 2 inches back from the front. Nail it in place through the sides. Place the other strip at the top, just above the top shelf and flush with the back. Nail it in place through the sides. If the sides will be visible, drive all of the nail heads below the surface with a nail set.

Improving Accuracy

When you cut bookcase parts with a jigsaw or a circular saw, it's difficult to be as accurate as you'd be if you used a large table saw—the professional's choice. With a belt sander, though, you can clean up the edges so that the top, bottom, and shelves all match and are square. Mark low points in the edges with squiggly pencil lines. Stack the parts, secure them with clamps, and then fine-tune the edges with a belt sander until the pencil lines just begin to disappear. Make light passes and hold the sander flat so you don't round the edges. Or place the clamped stack vertically on the floor and sand from above.

Building a plywood bookcase

Most built-in bookcases or other shelf units are made of plywood, particle-board, or MDF. Sheet materials are flat and easy to work with, and you don't have to worry about which way the material might cup. By matching hardwood plywood with hardwood trim of the same species, you can create built-in bookcases that look as if they are made of solid wood.

1 **RIP THE SIDES.** Clamp a straightedge along the length of a sheet of plywood (above, left) and cut a strip that matches the depth of the bookcase. Cut a matching piece.

2 **MEASURE AND RIP THE SHELVES.** Because this bookcase will have a back that's simply nailed on, the shelves are the same depth as the sides. Mark the width, then clamp on a straightedge and cut as you did the sides.

3 **SCORE AND CUT TO LENGTH.** To cut each side and shelf to length, clamp a straightedge over a piece at a right angle. Score the line with a sharp utility knife, then make the cut. If you are using a power miter saw or a table saw, you don't need to score first.

4 **MAKE A HOLE TEMPLATE.** Pegboard, the inexpensive perforated hardboard often used in garages for storage, makes a good template for spacing holes for 1/4-inch-diameter shelf pins. On both sides of the pegboard, draw circles around the holes you want, then note which end is going to be the top of the bookcase.

TOOL TIP

A Forstner bit, left, cuts the cleanest hole for shelf pins.

5 **MARK THE HOLES.** Position the template on one upright. With a 1/4-inch bit, preferably a Forstner type, drill a short distance into each marked hole, just enough to mark the locations. Use a block with a square edge as a guide if you're worried about drilling at an angle or too deep. Flip the template over, but keep the same edge pointing up as you mark hole locations for the other side of the upright. Repeat the procedure for the other upright.

6 **DRILL THE HOLES.** Put tape around the drill bit to mark the depth of the shelf pins. Remove the pegboard template and drill the holes to the proper depth. Watch the tape; when the "flag" sweeps away sawdust, the hole is the correct depth.

7 **ASSEMBLE THE FRAME.** On a flat work surface larger than the bookcase, set the sides on end. Ease the bottom or top in place. A clamp at the bottom helps keep pieces from tipping.

8 **ATTACH THE ENDS.** Snug a second clamp higher up, then remove the first one, so you have room to attach the pieces permanently. Predrill and countersink, then screw through the sides into the top or bottom. Secure the other end in the same way.

9 **ADD THE BACK.** Cut the back panel and place it on the bookcase frame. Don't worry if the sides angle out. Just align the bottom edge and screw the back in place there.

10 **SQUARE UP THE CASE.** Move to the other end of the bookcase and push or pull the parts until the back lines up with the frame. Screw the back in place. The case is complete, ready for you to fit with shelves and trim out as you wish. The bookcase shown here was destined to fit into a wall, as shown on pages 192–195. See page 218 for tips on how to build it in against a wall.

Recessing a bookcase into a wall

By fitting a bookcase or other cabinet into a wall, you can add storage space without significantly cutting into floor space. Shallow shelves may fit entirely within a wall. For a deeper cabinet, extend the front into the room a short distance, or nudge it farther back, into the adjoining room's space. In the project shown here, the cabinet did extend into the next room's closet, but the wall was opened up as if that weren't an option. This way, the procedure for avoiding damage to the back wall could be shown.

In most cases, recess cabinets only into interior walls. If you do decide to cut into an exterior wall, you will need to make up for the lost insulation, so the job becomes more complex. If you will be cutting studs, check with your local building office, as you may need a building permit. Also determine whether the wall is load-bearing (see below) and take appropriate precautions if it is.

This recessed cabinet takes advantage of the deep space needed for a neighboring closet. The result is a seven-drawer dresser that takes up none of the bedroom's floor space.

Recognizing a Load-Bearing Wall

Walls that run in the same direction as floor and ceiling joists don't usually carry a structural load, but ones that run crosswise often do. Even if a wall is load bearing, you can usually cut one stud without a problem, but you may need to brace the ceilings on both sides of the wall before you install a header, the horizontal framing at the top of the opening. If you're not sure about loads or bracing needs, consult a structural engineer or an experienced builder.

Here, a ceiling is being braced before a stud is removed in the adjacent wall. First, a smooth 2 × 4 that crosses under several ceiling joists is held against the ceiling. Then, two more 2 × 4s, cut slightly too long, are wedged between the 2 × 4 on the ceiling and a scrap of plywood on the floor.

1 **CHECK THE WALL.** With a hole saw, cut an inspection port so you can check for hidden wires or pipes. Twirl a bent wire around to feel for obstructions past the point where you can peer with the aid of a flashlight. Finding wires or pipes doesn't necessarily rule out recessing a cabinet, but it does complicate the job.

2 **MARK THE PERIMETER.** With a level and a pencil, outline the shape of the opening, plus enough space to maneuver in a header, if the wall is load bearing (see Step 9, page 194). If you already have a cabinet that you want to inset, slightly oversize the opening. Score the line with a sharp utility blade. Go over it several times, cutting deeper each time.

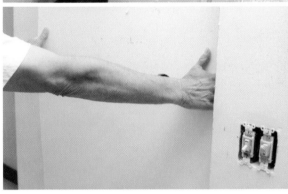

3 **PIVOT THE PANEL.** When you have cut through all the edges, rock the drywall back and forth. You'll probably see nails or screws pop loose where a stud lies underneath. Pull out the fasteners, and with a little more pushing and pulling you can probably pull out the panel in one piece.

4 **CUT THE STUDS.** With a reciprocating saw or a compass saw, cut a slot for the blade 1½ inches below the bottom of the opening. Saw through the studs there. Angle the blade so you don't cut through the drywall on the opposite wall. (This wall had two studs because of the closet on the far side.)

5 **LOOSEN THE NAILS.** Slip a pry bar or chisel behind the cut stud or studs to open a little space next to the drywall at the back. With a reciprocating saw or a hacksaw blade in a small handle, cut through the nails. If you're careful, you may be able to avoid any damage to that wall.

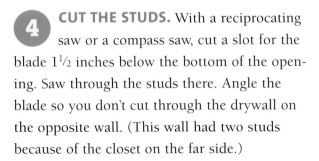

continued ▶▶

6 **REMOVE THE STUDS.** If the opening extends nearly to the ceiling, twist the studs free at the top. Use wire cutters to clip off any framing nails that hang down. If the opening is lower, cut studs at the top the way you did at the bottom.

7 **ADD CRIPPLE STUDS AND A SILL.** Cut short studs, known as cripples, so they reach to the bottom of the opening, minus $1\frac{1}{2}$ inches. They should match the height of the stud sections you cut. Cut a 2 × 4 that spans the opening, then nail or screw it across the cripples.

8 **CUT A HEADER AND A TRIMMER.** Cut a 2 × 6 header that's the width of the opening plus a hair. Hammer it into place. Screw at an angle to attach it to studs on the sides. Then cut a 2 × 4 trimmer the same length and install it sideways to trim out the top of the opening. On a load-bearing wall, sandwich two headers together. In any case, make sure you have left enough room vertically for your cabinet, if you are installing one that is already made.

9 **ADD TRIMMER STUDS.** On each side of the opening, install a vertical 2 × 4 between the sill and the top trimmer just behind the inside edge of the drywall. Screw these in place at the top and bottom.

PRO TRICK

Because the header and trimmer in Steps 8 and 9 must fit snugly, you'll need to cut off a bit of one corner of each piece so you can pivot it into position at the top.

10 **POSITION THE CABINET.** With one screw through the center, attach a short piece of shim material to each side of the opening and at the center on top. Muscle the cabinet into position.

11 **HOLD IT IN PLACE.** Pivot the sticks to keep the cabinet from falling out of the wall while you tuck shims between the case and the framing to level it. Insert one or more shelves as spacers to make sure the cabinet sides are not bowing in or out.

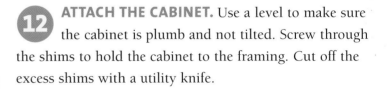

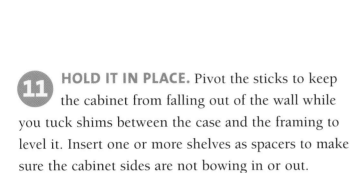

12 **ATTACH THE CABINET.** Use a level to make sure the cabinet is plumb and not tilted. Screw through the shims to hold the cabinet to the framing. Cut off the excess shims with a utility knife.

13 **ADD MOLDING.** Skirt the edges of the cabinet with molding that covers the exposed plywood layers and the gap with the drywall (for more about molding, see pages 218–221). You'll need pairs of nails—one to hold the molding to the cabinet and a second to secure the molding to the framing behind the drywall.

CUSTOM CABINETS

LIKE BOOKCASES, CABINETS ARE ESSENTIALLY JUST BOXES, but cabinets are usually equipped with doors and drawers in addition to shelves.

There are two main types: wall cabinets and base cabinets. Wall cabinets are supported on nail rails, generally 1 × 2s or 1 × 3s made of hardwood or void-free plywood. The nail rail should be placed at the back of a cabinet, flush with the underside of its top. Add a second rail at the bottom if the cabinet is large or will be filled with heavy items like ceramic dishes. Screw through the sides of the cabinet to attach the rail, then screw through the rail from inside to fasten the cabinet to wall studs.

Base cabinets, which sit on the floor and therefore don't need nail rails, usually support countertops, so the cabinet tops usually consist of just braces or corner blocks instead of finished panels. On cabinets that will be used as vanities, corner blocks leave plenty of free space in the middle for a sink.

Base cabinets usually have a bottom recess 3 inches deep and $3^1/2$ to $4^1/2$ inches high. Called a toe-kick, this detail allows you to stand close to the counter without bumping your feet. To incorporate a toe-kick into a base cabinet, notch the sides and cover the void with a strip $^3/4$ inches thick. Or build a kickbase separately. That's the easier approach if you have several base cabinets to install, because you can level the kickbases and then set the cabinets on top. Cabinets with notched bases need to be leveled individually.

Cabinet frame styles

Whether cabinets hang on a wall or sit on the floor, they can be divided into two more broad categories: face-frame and frameless. The type you choose determines your options for doors, drawers, and hinges.

- FACE-FRAME CABINETS have a wooden frame that masks the front edges of the cabinet box. Face-frame cabinets look most traditional, as older cabinets were always made this way. The frame is often built out of 1 × 2s held together with biscuit joinery or pocket screws (see page 201). Frame pieces have butt joints, not miters. If you build a face-frame cabinet, you can have inset doors and drawer fronts, which fit flush into the frame openings, or partial-overlay doors and drawer fronts, which cover the edge of the frame. One drawback of face-frames is that they reduce the size of the cabinet openings, which means drawers can't hold quite as much as those in frameless cabinets.

- FRAMELESS CABINETS have a more modern look. Drawers can extend across the full width of the cabinet, except for space occupied by drawer glides. But the space advantage does not apply to shelf storage behind doors. The Euro-style cup hinges usually found on these doors jut into the opening when a door pivots out, so the available space may be about the same as on face-frame cabinets.

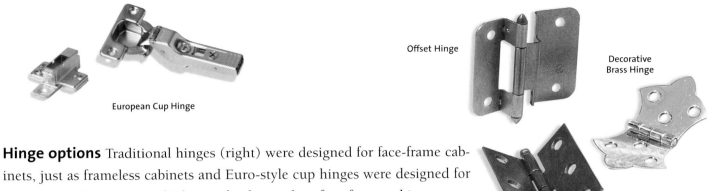

European Cup Hinge

Offset Hinge

Decorative
Brass Hinge

Butt Hinge

Hinge options Traditional hinges (right) were designed for face-frame cabinets, just as frameless cabinets and Euro-style cup hinges were designed for each other. Cup hinges, which can also be used on face-frame cabinets, are hidden when the doors are closed. The best ones are adjustable and clip on and off, so you can remove doors without a screwdriver.

Types of Cabinets

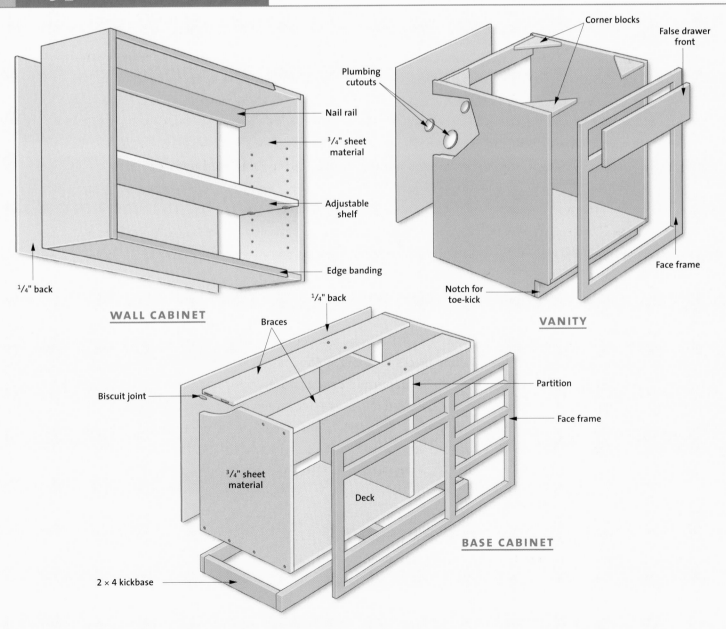

Corner blocks

False drawer
front

Plumbing
cutouts

Nail rail

³/₄" sheet
material

Adjustable
shelf

Edge banding

¹/₄" back

Face frame

Notch for
toe-kick

WALL CABINET

VANITY

¹/₄" back

Braces

Partition

Biscuit joint

Face frame

³/₄" sheet
material

Deck

BASE CABINET

2 × 4 kickbase

Building a wall cabinet

For a wall cabinet like the one illustrated on page 197, consider using melamine-coated particleboard. This material is inexpensive, doesn't require sanding or finishing, and has a wipe-clean surface. Melamine is sold in convenient widths. You may even find pieces pre-drilled to hold shelf supports. However, using this material does present some challenges. The coating tends to chip if you cut it with a standard blade, though you can prevent that (see Tool Tip at left). Also, the core material is standard particleboard, which doesn't hold fasteners as well as plywood does. Cut shallow rabbets that expose the particleboard core, then use screws and glue to hold joints together. Or, if you opt to just screw the components together, purchase screws designed to grip well in particleboard. Confirmat is one brand that is thicker and has coarser threads than regular wood screws.

1 **CUT AND RABBET.** Purchase $^3/_4$-inch-thick material that's the width you need for the cabinet frame and shelf, or rip pieces from a larger sheet. Crosscut the sides to height of the cabinet and then cut a $^1/_4$-inch-deep rabbet into each end. Crosscut the top and bottom pieces to the cabinet width minus 1 inch. Cut the shelves $^1/_2$ inch shorter. On the top, bottom, and sides, cut a $^1/_4$-inch-deep rabbet along the back edge so that the cabinet back is flush. Cut a back panel from $^1/_4$-inch-thick material.

2 **ASSEMBLE THE CASE.** On a wide work surface, set the top, bottom, and sides in place, with one clamp on each end. Check that the case is square, then drill holes for $1^5/_8$-inch particleboard screws. Remove the clamps, apply wood glue, reposition the clamps, and screw the case together.

3 **ADD THE BACK.** Turn over the case, check the back for fit, then nail it in place with 1-inch headed brads every 8 inches or so. Also use glue if you wish.

4 **INSTALL THE NAIL RAIL.** Cut a strip of maple or other hardwood for the nail rail (top right). Make it $^3/_4$ inch thick, about 2 inches wide, and the exact width of the cabinet interior. Drill holes through the sides, then drive finish nails (or screws if appearance doesn't matter).

5 **ADD EDGING.** Cover the raw particleboard edges of the case and shelf with strips of solid wood or iron-on edging, as shown on page 169.

A wall cabinet with cleats instead of rails

If you don't want a nail rail on the interior of your cabinet, you can recess the back of the cabinet by the thickness of the back piece plus ¾ inch, then install the rail behind the back. If you take this approach, you can simplify the installation by cutting a rail and a ledger with angled edges that mate to each other. This frees you from having to keep the cabinet steady and level while you screw it into studs. Instead, you screw the ledger to the wall so it's level, then lift the cabinet into place.

1 RECESS THE BACK. If you are using a ¼-inch-thick back and ¾-inch-thick hardwood or plywood rails, cut a rabbet 1 inch deep along the back edge of the sides, top, and bottom. Use a router or a table saw with a dado blade. If you don't have a dado blade, cut the recess in two steps with a table saw fitted with a zero-clearance (tight-fitting) throat plate. First cut 1 inch deep along the edge. Use a featherboard to help ensure an even cut. Then flip the board on its side to make a shallower cut to remove the strip. Position the rip fence so the strip falls away on the outside of the blade, not next to the fence.

2 MAKE THE RAIL AND LEDGER. From a piece of knot-free hardwood or void-free plywood that's ¾ inch thick, cut a strip about 5½ inches wide that fits snugly between the cabinet sides. Adjust a table saw blade to cut at a 45-degree angle, then rip the strip in half.

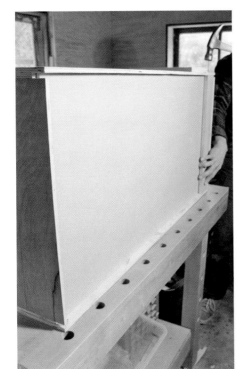

3 ATTACH THE RAIL. Align one piece at the back of the cabinet so the angled tip will face down and out when the cabinet is hanging. Nail or screw through the cabinet sides to attach the rail.

4 INSTALL THE CABINET. Draw a level line on the wall where the bottom of the ledger should be. Locate studs. Place the ledger along the line and then screw through the ledger into the studs. The ledger's bevel tip should point up and out. If there aren't at least two studs behind the cabinet, install the ledger with drywall anchors, as shown in Step 10 on page 184.

Building a base cabinet

It's possible to build a base cabinet with simple screwed-together corners, as shown for the bookcase on pages 198–199. But for a stronger cabinet, consider using biscuit joinery in addition. The cabinet shown here (and illustrated on page 197) includes a partition and spaces for drawers, a typical configuration for a vanity, but the design is easy to change. For example, you could build two cabinets and put the drawers in one. Or, for a frameless cabinet, you could skip the face frame and apply wood or iron-on edging to the front.

1 CUT THE PIECES. Cut out the parts using the procedure shown on page 190 if you're using a jigsaw or a circular saw. The sides, vertical partition, and deck (bottom) are all the same width, but the partition is shorter than the sides because it fits over the deck and under the top braces. The top braces and the deck are the same length. Cut slots for biscuits into the ends of the deck, the partition, and the braces. Make matching slots in the face of the side panels near the top and bottom. Also cut slots in the bottom and the top braces where the partition will stand. Keeping track of which slots go where can be confusing. A sketch helps.

2 TEST AND GLUE. Recruit a helper for this and the next two steps, if possible. Assemble the parts dry to test the fit and assembly order. Then take apart the pieces and reassemble them with glue. Spread glue in the slots on the deck and then slip in the biscuits. Apply glue to the matching slots on the sides and partition. With the deck upright on its back edge, press the sides and partition in place against the bottom. Secure each joint with self-piloting screws driven through the outside, but avoid screwing through the biscuits.

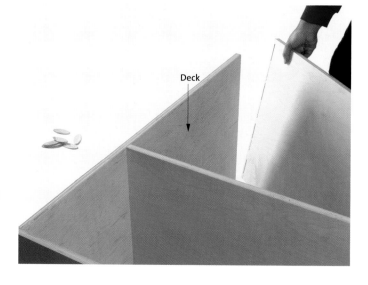

Deck

3 ADD BRACES. Carefully rotate the cabinet so the top edges face up. Add glue to the top slots and to the corresponding slots on the top braces. Insert the biscuits and press the parts together. One brace should be flush with the front edge, the other with the back edge. Drive screws into the vertical partition and into the ends of the braces to keep them tight.

4 **ADD THE BACK.** Rotate the case again so the front faces down. Set the back in place. Nail or screw one edge. Then, since the back is square, use it to square up the cabinet. Push or pull on the sides until the frame lines up with the back. Nail or screw down the remaining edges. To make sure you nail into the center of the vertical partition, snap a chalk line.

DESIGN TIP

A face frame often looks best when its sides are more slender than its top and bottom. For example, you might want 1 × 2s for the sides but 1 × 3s for the top and bottom. Wider horizontals also allow you to use common biscuit sizes.

5 **MAKE THE FACE FRAME.** Select solid, knot-free wood $3/4$ inch thick by at least $1^{1}/_{2}$ inches wide. Use pieces with square edges, as rounded edges don't make tight-looking joints. Though the frame needs to be only as wide as the outside of the cabinet, you might want to make it bigger so that the frame and cabinet box are flush on the inside edge but the frame overlaps on the outside. Then you can use the overhangs as scribing strips when you install the cabinet. For frame joints, use biscuit joinery or drive screws through the joints at an angle. These angled screws are often called pocket screws because they fit into recessed pilot holes, or pockets, that you drill with the aid of a special jig. Follow instructions that come with the jig.

6 **INSTALL THE FACE FRAME.** Spread glue on the front of the box and set the face frame over that. Check the alignment to make sure it's square with the cabinet. Before you secure it with finish nails, drill pilot holes with a bit that's skinnier than the nails.

If you find a recycled cabinet that's too narrow for your space, consider stretching its look by adding shelves to one or both ends. Besides making the cabinet appear more like it was custom-built for the wall, the shelves will add storage space.

Recycling and adapting for built-ins

Finding used cabinets that are precisely the right size for your built-in project isn't easy, but there are many ways to adapt ones that are too small or too big. If the cabinets are too small, plug gaps with filler strips or add other features, such as spice drawers, shelves, or cubbyholes for storing trays, a card table, a fold-up stepstool, or other items. If the cabinets are too big, you may be able to modify them.

• CABINET BOXES are easy to shorten or make less deep (see pages 204–205).

• DRAWERS are especially easy to shorten if they have a false front. Drawer heights aren't as simple to change.

• DOORS can be easy or difficult to alter, depending on the type. With a flat-panel door, the only real challenge is matching the edging. With a frame-and-panel door, you can trim small amounts from the length and width, but major changes could weaken the door and leave it looking out of proportion.

• SHELVES are easy to shorten. But before you cut, see the tips on page 175 to make sure you allow for any out-of-square angles.

Wall cabinets are usually not as deep as base cabinets, and they need not be as wide. Wall cabinets that are a bit smaller than their companion base cabinets feel less top-heavy and looming in a room.

If you use a cabinet as a base for a desk, you have a lot of leeway on how wide an opening to leave for the chair. Installing an edge band between the countertop and the wall conceals any gaps that might exist there.

ABOVE: When there is a gap at least 6 inches wide, consider adding a cabinet with small drawers or narrow shelves. A cabinet that's taller, shorter, or skinnier than the others is distinctive enough that it doesn't need to match.

Skinny pullout storage units put spaces as narrow as 3¹/₂ inches to good use. Options include a towel rack (far right) and spice shelves (right). Cabinet companies make these pullouts with front panels that match other cabinet details, or you can make your own. Use full-extension drawer glides at the top, bottom, or both.

Turning a $10 castoff into a built-in

The project shown here transformed an unused alcove under an eave into a useful storage area. The built-in began as a used cabinet that cost just $10 because it was missing the decorative panel on its top drawer. Otherwise, the piece was in good shape. But it was too tall and too narrow for the space, so the challenge was to adapt it to fit. The solution was to shorten the cabinet at the top and add new shelves on the right.

1 **DECIDE WHERE TO TRIM.** For this transformation, the cabinet box was shortened by one drawer. Trimming from the top is always easiest in a case like this because it leaves the toe-kick detail intact. Screw or clamp a straightedge at the appropriate height, then score along the line with a utility blade to minimize splintering when you cut. Before you cut, remove the drawer glide on the inside of the cabinet.

This castoff $10 cabinet box, with three sets of drawers and slides, was a good candidate for a built-in. A big plus was the oak drawer fronts. Besides being in good shape, they were easy to modify and covered big gaps between the drawer boxes, which made it easy to adjust the drawer spacing from three to two.

2 **MAKE THE CUTS.** Clamp a temporary spacer between the two sides of the cabinet box so it doesn't collapse when you cut off its top portion. With a circular saw or a jigsaw, make the cut. Repeat on the opposite side and the back. Then remove the stretcher bar that was at the top in the front and the corner blocks in the back and reinstall them on the shortened cabinet.

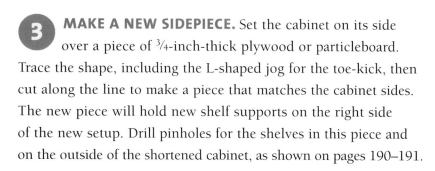

3 **MAKE A NEW SIDEPIECE.** Set the cabinet on its side over a piece of ¾-inch-thick plywood or particleboard. Trace the shape, including the L-shaped jog for the toe-kick, then cut along the line to make a piece that matches the cabinet sides. The new piece will hold new shelf supports on the right side of the new setup. Drill pinholes for the shelves in this piece and on the outside of the shortened cabinet, as shown on pages 190–191.

4 **ADJUST THE DRAWER GLIDES.** Move the drawer glides to accommodate the new height of the cabinet. To make sure the glides wind up equally high and perfectly level, cut a scrap piece of wood to the height of the bottom of the top glide. Screw the glide in place with it resting on the scrap piece. Then move the piece to the opposite side of the cabinet and install the other glide. Trim the scrap to the drawer height below, and repeat the steps.

5 **MODIFY THE DRAWER FRONTS.** Slide the drawer boxes into the cabinet and then clamp the front panels on. Decide where to trim them so they don't overlap and so the top piece overlaps all but about $1/8$ inch of the top of the cabinet. In this case, it was easiest to trim the bottoms of the drawer fronts. Allow for a $1/8$-inch space between the drawer fronts.

6 **MAKE NEW SHELVES AND TOE-KICK.** To fill in the remaining width of the opening in the setup, cut as many shelves as you want, plus one piece for the bottom. Also cut a toe-kick cover and a countertop piece that span the full width. To cover the front edges of all of these pieces, apply iron-on veneer, as shown on page 169.

7 **INSTALL THE PIECES.** Move the cabinet into place and screw through one side into wall studs. On the opposite wall, attach the new sidepiece. Set the countertop on the cabinet and sidepiece, then secure it with screws or finish nails. Add the toe-kick cover. Apply double-stick tape to the fronts of the drawer boxes. Place the upper one into position.

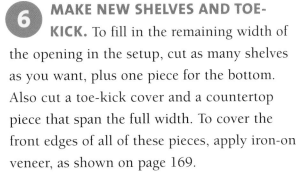

8 **FINAL DETAILS.** Place a spacer $1/8$ inch thick between the drawer fronts as you push the lower one into place against the tape. Open the drawer carefully and screw through the drawer boxes into the drawer fronts. Slide the shelves into place, then add a length of solid wood trim to mask the plywood edge on the countertop.

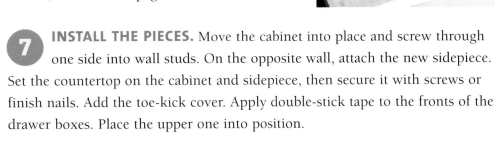

CABINET DOORS

STUDY THE DOORS ON CABINETS and other built-ins and you'll quickly see that they divide into three types: flat doors made from a single sheet of plywood or MDF; frame-and-panel doors, in which a wood frame surrounds a wood panel; and board-and-batten doors, which consist of parallel boards screwed or nailed to braces on the back.

Flat doors Flat doors are simplest to make. Plywood is strong and is a stable material for hinges, but MDF stays flatter. If you want a clear finish, cut your piece from a thick sheet of finished plywood ($3/4$ inch is standard), or add veneer to both sides of MDF. The plywood grain on flat doors typically runs vertically. For edging, use strips of solid wood or iron-on veneer tape, or a combination of the two. If you want a painted door, MDF is the best choice because it takes paint well and doesn't need edging.

Frame-and-panel doors Frame-and-panel doors evolved from cabinetmakers' need to deal with the expansion and contraction that occurs in solid wood, which was once the only material they had to work with. There are three basic styles for the center panel: flat, raised bevel (also called raised panel), and square shoulder. If you want a clear finish for your doors, use plywood for flat panels and use solid wood for raised or square shoulder panels. To minimize the warping of solid wood, use boards less than 6 inches wide and edge-glue them together with the grain curving in alternating directions. If you plan to paint your doors, MDF is a good choice for the center panel, regardless of the style.

To secure the panel in the frame, cut a rabbet or a dado along the inside edges of the frame. Either option is fine if panels are plywood or MDF, but solid wood needs dadoes so the panels have a way to expand and contract as humidity changes. Glass panels should be in rabbets so you can replace the glass if it breaks.

To join frame pieces, use butt joints reinforced with hidden dowels or biscuits, or cut tongue-and-groove or mortise-and-tenon joints. Biscuit joints are easiest, but you might need wide rails so the slots cut for the biscuits don't show. Tongue-and-groove joints are usually made with a table saw and a dado set. Rail-and-stile joints are easiest to make with a router on a router table.

Board-and-batten doors These doors are enjoying a renaissance among people who want a distinctly non-manufactured look in their homes. Panels are often assembled of tongue-and-groove boards, which accommodate the seasonal shrinking and swelling that occurs in solid wood. Two horizontal braces on the back are enough for short doors, but tall ones need a diagonal brace as well. See the project on page 210.

Door Designs

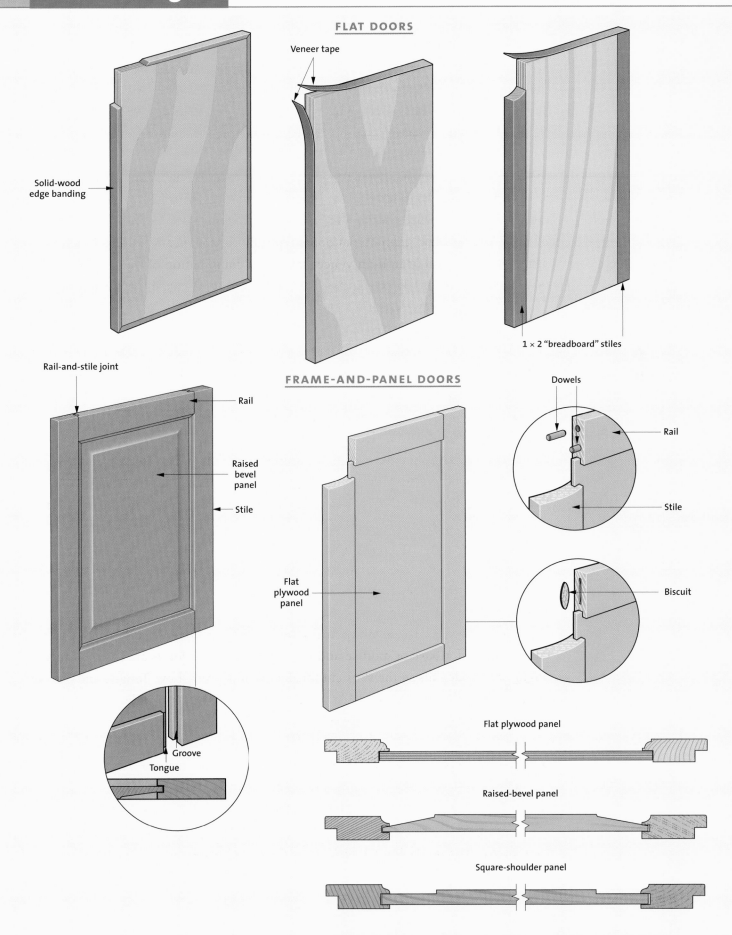

FLAT DOORS

Veneer tape

Solid-wood edge banding

1 × 2 "breadboard" stiles

Rail-and-stile joint

Rail

Raised bevel panel

Stile

FRAME-AND-PANEL DOORS

Dowels

Rail

Stile

Flat plywood panel

Biscuit

Groove

Tongue

Flat plywood panel

Raised-bevel panel

Square-shoulder panel

Building a flat-panel door

You'll need a table saw to make this basic frame-and-panel door and a dado set helps, but you won't need to buy any expensive bits or do any complicated joinery. Because the frame will be painted, it is made of poplar, $3/4$ inch thick by $2\frac{1}{2}$ inches wide, and the center panel is made of $1/4$-inch-thick MDF, which stays flatter than most types of $1/4$-inch plywood.

Cut the stiles, or vertical frame pieces, so they equal the height of the door. Calculate the length of the rails, or crosspieces, by subtracting the width of the two stiles and then adding 1 inch, to account for the $1/2$-inch-long tongues you will form on each rail end.

Make the center panel as wide as the rails are long, plus $15/16$ inch so that the panel will fit into grooves you cut in the stiles. This creates a gap of $1/16$ inch so the MDF can expand and contract freely as humidity levels change. The height of the panel should equal the door height minus the width of two rails, plus $15/16$ inch.

1 ADJUST THE SAW. Install a zero-clearance (tight-fitting) plate on a table saw and raise the blade $1/2$ inch high. Set the fence so it's slightly more than $1/4$ inch from the inside of the blade. Clamp on a featherboard to apply sideways pressure when the frame pieces are set on edge against the fence. To cut a groove, run a test piece that's the same thickness as the frame over the blade.

2 CUT THE GROOVE. Turn the test piece around and run it past the blade with the opposite face pointing toward the fence. Check whether this widens the groove enough for the center panel to fit snugly. If it does not, make another test piece, adjust the fence as needed, and try again. Depending on the width of your saw blade, you may need to readjust the fence and make a third pass to remove the sliver of wood at the center of the groove.

3 MAKE RAIL TONGUES. Lower the blade so it's as high as the width of the shoulders on either side of the groove. Place a stop block against the rip fence and adjust it so the block is $1/2$ inch from the blade. Clamp the block to the end of the rip fence and switch on the saw. Position a test piece so one end is against the stop block and one edge is against the miter gauge. Holding the piece firmly against the miter gauge, move it past the blade. Check to see whether this cut matches the depth of the grooves. If it does not, readjust the fence. When the fit is right, run both sides of each rail's end past the blade. After the first cuts, reposition the rail against the miter gauge so the end is about a blade's width away from the stop block, then make a second cut. Repeat as necessary to remove all of the shoulder on the last $1/2$ inch of the rail. You should wind up with tongues that fit snugly into the grooves on the stiles.

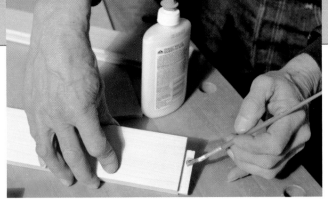

4 **CHECK THE FIT, THEN GLUE.** Assemble the door without glue to make sure all the parts fit well. Mark where the panel fits into the stiles and take the pieces apart. Where the frame pieces meet, spread glue in the groove of one stile and on the stile's shoulders as well as on the tongue and surrounding surface of one rail. Push the rail and stile together, slip the panel in, and glue the other rail and stile junctions in the same way.

5 **CLAMP AND CHECK.** Adjust clamps so they press the stiles to the ends of the rails. Measure diagonally across the door in both directions. If the measurements are equal, the door is square. If not, loosen the clamps, readjust the parts as needed, and re-clamp.

Solid Wood Panels

Using solid wood for the center panel is trickier than using sheet material because solid wood shrinks and swells with humidity. If you want solid wood, you'll need to edge-glue boards together to create a bigger piece—each board should be no wider than 6 inches. If your door will be wider than $13^3/_4$ inches, redesign it so that it includes two small side-by-side panels, with an extra stile between them.

Cut solid-wood panels up to $^1/_2$ inch narrower than you would an MDF panel, and make the grooves in the stiles and rails a little loose. To keep the panel from rattling, slip weather stripping or plastic fillers known as space balls into the grooves before you add the panel and glue the door-frame pieces together. If you plan to paint or stain the door, apply the finish before you put everything together.

6 **MAKE SURE THE DOOR IS FLAT.** With a straight-edge, check the door in all directions to make sure it is flat. If it's not, place two thick, straight boards on top. Slightly loosen the end clamps, then clamp the flat boards down and retighten the end clamps. Wipe away any excess glue with a damp cloth.

Building a board-and-batten door

One of the oldest types of doors, a board-and-batten door is also one of the easiest to build. Three tongue-and-groove pine boards were used for each of these doors, but you could use any other kind of boards that interlock. Make sure the boards are perfectly flat and straight or you'll wind up with doors that don't close properly. And to give the door a finished look, cut off or plug tongues or grooves on the exposed edges of the door's outside boards.

1 **CUT THE BOARDS.** Place the boards side by side, butted closely if you live in a dry climate or loosely if your region's average relative humidity is high. Measure in from the tongue or groove on each end board, then divide any excess width by 2. That is the amount to rip from the outside boards. The boards for these doors were so close to the correct width that ripping the groove and bevel from the outside board would have made the door too skinny. Instead, the groove was plugged with tongue pieces ripped from boards that were used to make the braces, and then the tongue on the door's other side was trimmed to fit.

Z-shaped bracing helps keep board-and-batten doors from sagging. The brace should always slant down toward the hinge.

2 **ADD BRACES AND DIAGONAL.** To determine the width of the cross braces, set a hinge in place to show the gap needed on one side; leave an equal setback on the other side. Bevel the ends of the braces, then screw them to the boards, using one or two screws in each middle board and two or three in each end board. Attach the diagonal in the same way, with its bottom end near the bottom hinge.

3 **ATTACH THE HINGES.** These doors have overlay hinges, which attach to the back of the door. A self-centering punch or drill bit makes a pilot hole perfectly centered in the space.

4 **POSITION THE DOORS.** Place the doors in the cabinet opening and align them so they are level and have an equal gap at the middle. This cabinet was built into a recessed opening in a wall, so a scrap piece of plywood was placed underneath the doors to provide temporary support.

5 **APPLY FINAL TOUCHES.** Screw the hinges to the cabinet frame or molding, then add handles or latches to keep the doors closed.

Building a glass-panel door

This project features a maple frame that's ¾ inch thick by 2½ inches wide, with a ⅛-inch-thick tempered-glass center panel. Two ⁵⁄₁₆-by-2-inch dowels reinforce each corner of the frame. Drilling by hand is tricky, but by assembling the door before you cut the groove for the glass, you can sand off any irregularities. Use dowels with grooved sides, which come in short lengths.

1   BORE HOLES. To bore holes for the dowels, you'll need a doweling jig (shown) or a drill press. Lay out the cut frame pieces and draw pencil marks that show the center of the dowels. Label the pieces in pencil so you can match them later. Position the jig and then drill each hole a little deeper than 1 inch. Mark the depth by wrapping the drill bit in tape, or use a depth stop.

2   ASSEMBLE THE FRAME. Test the fit and adjust clamps to pull the joints tight. Then pull or tap the frame apart and pull the dowels out with pliers. Apply glue to the holes and spread a little more on the shoulders where framing pieces butt together. Push the joints together again and cinch them tight with the clamps. Use a straightedge to be sure the clamps aren't causing the door to bow, then measure the door diagonally both ways. Equal measurements mean the door is square. If it's not, loosen the clamps, adjust the sides, and retighten the clamps. Wipe off excess glue with a moist cloth.

3   CUT RABBETS. The next day, sand any uneven joints. Clamp the frame to a workbench. Tighten a self-piloting rabbet bit into a router and adjust the depth to be equal to, or a little deeper than, the thickness of the glass. Place the router on the frame, with the bit away from the wood. Switch the motor on and move the router clockwise as you press the bit against the wood. After the cut is complete, square up the rounded corners with a wood chisel.

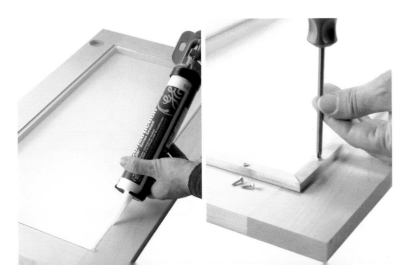

4   ADD THE GLASS. Squirt a small bead of glazing sealant along the rabbet. Add the glass. Cover the edges by screwing on wooden molding. Use molding that's wide enough so the screws don't hit and crack the glass.

CABINET DRAWERS

DRAWERS MADE THE TRADITIONAL WAY, with interlocking joints at corners and a bottom enclosed in a groove, are among the more challenging built-in components to make. Not only must you accurately size, cut, and join numerous pieces, but you also need to make sure the drawers fit precisely in a cabinet recess.

Traditional drawers consist of five parts: a front, a back, two sides and a bottom. Many modern drawers have a sixth piece: a decorative front panel, also known as a false front, which is screwed to the front of the drawer box. A false front makes it easy to hide drawer-glide hardware and to line up drawer fronts.

PLYWOOD DRAWER

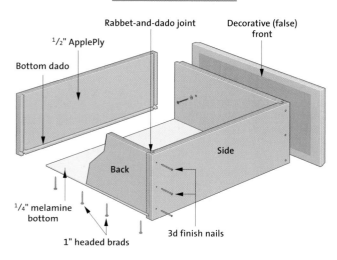

Rabbet-and-dado joint

½" ApplePly

Bottom dado

Decorative (false) front

Side

Back

¼" melamine bottom

1" headed brads

3d finish nails

DOVETAIL DRAWER

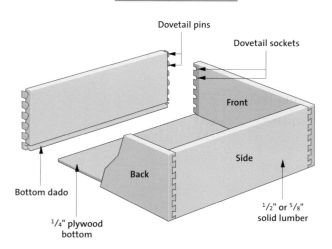

Dovetail pins

Dovetail sockets

Front

Side

Back

Bottom dado

¼" plywood bottom

½" or ⅝" solid lumber

Matching materials and construction methods

Although drawers have been made from solid wood for years, increasingly they tend to be made from sheet materials. One of the easiest materials to work with is ½-inch hardwood plywood often sold as Baltic birch or ApplePly. A strong, veneer core material with numerous void-free layers, it's attractive enough that you can simply round over the edges and leave them exposed on drawer sides. Melamine-coated particleboard at least ⅝ inch thick is another option, but the drawers won't be as strong and you'll almost certainly want to cover the edges with iron-on tape. If you want to make dovetailed drawers with joints cut by hand or with a router and a jig, solid wood like poplar or pine is best.

Drawer bottoms are often made of ¼-inch-thick hardboard, melamine-coated hardboard, or hardwood plywood. Material this thin needs to be supported by a groove cut into the drawer's inside surfaces. The groove can extend all the way around the drawer box. Or, for easier assembly, run the groove only along the sides and front, and nail the bottom to the back edge. If you opt to make the drawer bottom ½ inch thick, you can skip the groove entirely and just nail or screw the bottom to the box (see opposite page).

Choosing drawer guides

For the smoothest, most trouble-free drawer action, choose prefabricated metal guide sets that attach to drawer bottoms or sides. If you decide to nail or screw the bottom panel to the drawer rather than set it in a groove, choose the standard type of bottom-mount drawer guides. They'll cover the edges of the drawer bottom so you won't see it on the sides when you open the drawer. If you are building a drawer with a set-in bottom, you also have the option of a newer kind of bottom-mount guide that fits under the bottom panel so that the guide itself doesn't show.

Most guides extend only three-quarters of their length. Full-extension guides allow the drawer to slide out completely. They cost more but are worthwhile on drawers used for tall items, such as pots or file folders.

Building a simple drawer

You might not win an old-time woodworker's praise for doing so, but you can build a serviceable drawer with simple tools by constructing a basic box with just butt joints that are glued and nailed or screwed together. Add a false front and you've got a perfectly good-looking drawer.

The bottom of this drawer is nailed directly to the sides rather than set in a groove. Attaching the bottom this way strengthens the box and turns it into essentially a sliding shelf. Use standard bottom-mount guides. They typically require $1/2$-inch clearance on each side, so make the drawer box 1 inch narrower than the cabinet opening.

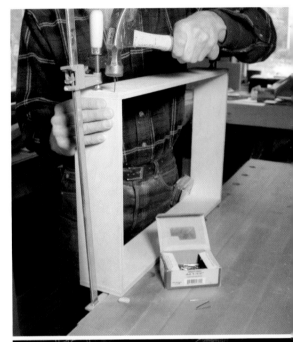

1 **ASSEMBLE THE BOX.** The front and back drawer pieces fit between the sides. Spread glue where these pieces meet, then drive fasteners through the sides into the front and back. Use $1^{1}/_4$- or $1^{1}/_2$-inch-long finish nails (3d or 4d). If you have trouble driving them straight, drill pilot holes with a bit that's skinnier than the nails. Switch to $2^{1}/_4$-inch nails or screws for $3/4$-inch-thick solid wood or plywood. For $5/8$-inch-thick material, such as melamine-coated particleboard, use 2-inch particleboard screws.

2 **ADD THE BOTTOM.** Set the drawer box upside down. Spread glue on the edge at the top, then lower the bottom panel onto that. Fasten one edge, then push or pull on other edges of the box to square it up with the bottom. Attach the remaining edges with the same kind of fasteners you used on the sides. Wipe off excess glue with a damp cloth.

3 **INSTALL THE GUIDES.** Attach bottom-mount drawer guides as specified in the manufacturer's instructions. See page 205 for details on how to install the mating pieces in the cabinet and how to attach a decorative front piece.

Building a drawer with a set-in bottom

With a table saw or a router, you can build a drawer with interlocking joinery and a set-in bottom. The sides of the drawer shown here are $1/2$-inch-thick void-free plywood. The bottom is $1/4$-inch-thick melamine-coated hardboard. The bottom slides into a groove on three sides and is nailed to the back of the drawer.

As on the simple drawer on page 213, the sides of this one are as long as the drawer box. If you are using $1/2$-inch-thick material and cut $1/4$-inch-deep vertical dadoes into the sides, the front and back pieces are the finished width minus $1/2$ inch. (Don't forget to allow clearance for drawer guides when you determine the width of the drawer box.) Make the front as high as the sides, but shorten the back by $5/8$ inch to allow the bottom to slide underneath it. The bottom should be $1/4$ inch shorter and $1/2$ inch narrower than the finished drawer box.

① **CUT DADOES.** With a table saw or a router, cut vertical grooves $1/4$ inch deep and wide on the side pieces. Make cuts on the inside, $1/4$ inch from the ends. Rabbet the front and back pieces to produce matching tongues. On the bottom edges of the sides and front, cut grooves $1/4$ inch deep and wide, and $3/8$ inch up from the bottom. If you are using a table saw, use a standard blade and make a couple of passes, or use a dado blade. For router cuts, use a straight bit and a router table.

② **ASSEMBLE THE BOX.** Spread wood glue in the vertical grooves and along the tongues that connect the sides to the front and back. Push the pieces together and drive $1 1/4$- or $1 1/2$-inch finish nails (3d or 4d) through the sides. If you find it hard to drive the nails straight in, drill first with a bit that's smaller than the nail diameter, then drive the nails. Finish with a nail set.

③ **ATTACH THE BOTTOM.** Slide the bottom into the grooves in the sides and front. You may need to tap the back edge with a hammer to seat the piece fully in the front groove. Check the box with a carpenter's square. Push or pull on the sides to square up the box, then nail the bottom to the lower edge of the back using 1-inch headed brads.

Building a dovetail drawer

With a dovetail jig and a router equipped with an appropriate bit, you can cut blind dovetails, which are very strong joints that don't show on the front of the drawer. This is the ideal fastening method if you want a one-piece drawer front and are using at least $1/2$-inch-thick solid wood for the drawer box. The drawer shown here has a bottom fully set into a groove, so the drawer needs to be assembled all at once—you can't add the bottom after you assemble the frame.

The front, back, and sides of the drawer box are equally high but vary in length. To determine the length of the sides, make a sample dovetail joint using your jig and router bit and material that matches the thickness of the drawer sides. Measure the shoulder that's free of dovetails on the end. Double that measurement and subtract it from the drawer box depth; that's the length of the sides. The front and back are simply as long as the drawer is wide. Cut the drawer bottom to the size of the finished drawer box, minus $7/16$ inch in length and width.

1 **CUT DOVETAILS.** Cut the dovetail pins and sockets, following the instructions that came with your dovetail jig. The pins on the sides should angle out toward the front and back, so that the drawer comes apart only from sideways pressure, not from tugging on the front.

2 **CUT DADOES.** Make grooves $1/4$ inch deep and wide along the inside lower edge of the sides, front, and back. Start the groove $3/8$ inch up from the bottom edge. Test the fit by slipping a scrap of the bottom material into the groove; it should slide in easily.

3 **ASSEMBLE THE BOX.** Put the parts together without glue. If they all fit, take them apart and spread wood glue inside the dovetail sockets and around the pins. Align one side and the front or back, then slip in the drawer bottom and fit the other pieces around it. You may need to tap on the sides to seat the dovetails. Check that the corners are square. If they are not, rack the box and check again. When the shape is correct, tighten a pair of clamps across the drawer. Then add a second pair perpendicular to the first. Wipe away excess glue with a damp cloth.

4 **TOUCH UP.** When the glue dries, touch up the top edge and the sides with a sander. Install the drawer as shown on page 205, but skip details about adding a false front if your cabinet design calls for a one-piece drawer front.

INSTALLING CABINETS

WHETHER YOU ARE INSTALLING A SINGLE CABINET or ganging several together to create a built-in wall system, desk, or other feature, you can usually get the job done with just a few basic tools: some clamps, a hammer, a drill, and a level.

If you are installing both base and wall cabinets, mark the wall for all the parts before you begin. Installing base cabinets first often makes the most sense, but if the wall pieces are extremely heavy, you might want to install them first before the base cabinets get in the way.

Installing base cabinets

Remove any baseboards or molding in your work area. Locate the wall studs by using a stud sensor, or drill pilot holes in areas that will be covered up later. If your cabinets have a built-in toe-kick, measure the exact cabinet height up from the floor in several spots. With a level, determine which mark is highest. Using that as your reference point, draw a level line across the wall. Shim and level each base so the cabinet reaches that line.

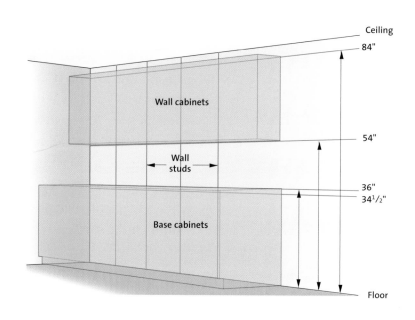

Ceiling
84"
Wall cabinets
54"
Wall studs
36"
34½"
Base cabinets
Floor

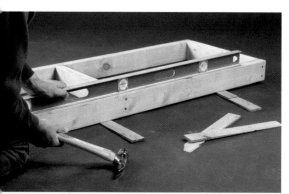

1 **BUILD A BASE.** If your cabinets are designed to sit on a kickbase, build a frame of 2 × 4 lumber or ³/₄-inch-thick plywood. The frame should be the same width as the cabinet, but it should be less deep by 3³/₄ inches to account for the toe-kick. Shim the kickbase as needed to make it level from side to side and front to back. Drive screws though the frame and shims into wall studs or floor joists. Trim the shims and cover the base with mitered trim or plywood facing strips.

2 **POSITION THE CABINET.** Cut any access holes you need on the cabinet's back, bottom, or top for plumbing pipes, wiring, sinks, or other features. Then lift the cabinet into position on the kickbase. If you are installing separate cabinet boxes side by side, clamp the front edges or face frames together. After they are aligned, drill countersink holes and screw the cabinets or face frames together.

3 **SCRIBE THE ENDS.** Where a cabinet meets a wall, scribe a trim strip (use the face frame itself if it's wide enough) to follow the shape of the wall. To scribe, position the strip or cabinet as close to the wall as you can, adjust a compass so the distance between the point and the pencil matches the widest gap between the strip and the wall, and run the compass down the wall to mark the board. Trim the strip to the line with a jigsaw, hand plane, or belt sander. Angle the cut so the front edge is narrow in case you need to fine-tune the fit.

4 **ATTACH THE CABINET.** Attach the trim strip, then screw through the cabinet's back rail with screws that are long enough to pass through the rail and drywall and still reach at least 1 inch into the studs. If the wall bows, use a shim to fill the gap and then drive the screw through the shim.

Installing wall cabinets

The main difference between wall cabinets and base cabinets is that when you are installing wall cabinets, gravity is no longer your friend. Measure up from the floor (or the top of base cabinets, if they are already in place) and mark the bottom edge of the wall cabinets, typically 54 inches from the floor. Because the floor may not be level, measure up in several places and use the highest or lowest mark as your reference point. Draw a level line at that height across the wall, using a carpenter's level as a straight-edge. Find the studs, transfer their locations to the cabinets, and drill pilot holes through the nail rails in the appropriate places.

Just below the level line on the wall, screw a 2 × 4 ledger temporarily to each stud. With a helper or two, lift one cabinet onto this support strip and brace it while you drive 3-inch wood screws through the nail rail into the studs (do not use drywall screws, as they are too brittle). Leave the screws a little loose. Install adjacent cabinets and add shims where necessary so all cabinets are level and plumb. Then screw the fronts of the cabinets, or their face frames, together. Finally, tighten all of the screws that hold the cabinets to the wall. Remove the temporary ledger and patch the wall.

LEVELING TIP

Instead of building a solid base, you can rest cabinets that don't have a built-in toe-kick on leveling legs, which can be adjusted to different heights. Leave these legs exposed if you like their look, or cover them later with a trim strip screwed or nailed to the bottom of the cabinet.

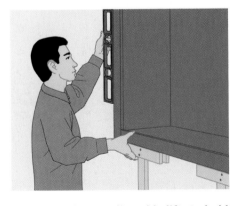

Professionals use adjustable lifts to hold the fronts of wall cabinets in position, but you can improvise with homemade T braces made from framing scraps. Use them to check that the cabinet is level and plumb. Even with braces, it's a good idea to have a helper nearby to keep the cabinet steady.

FINISHING TOUCHES

MOLDINGS AND OTHER TRIM are the final flourishes that make built-in projects look truly built in. They can mimic the look of other trim in the room or establish a distinctly different style. Moldings come in a wide range of profiles, including crown molding, baseboard, and window and door trim. You can also buy salvaged period pieces, as well as reproductions of pediments, mantels, and pilasters.

Style and material choices If you want to make a built-in blend into a room, take style cues from elements nearby. You don't necessarily need to match every detail—in a room with elaborate crown molding, for example, you might choose a more streamlined version to crown a built-in bookcase. Or you can move in the opposite direction and dress up the molding on a built-in so that the piece becomes the star attraction.

For projects with clear finishes, buy molding cut from a single piece. If you plan to paint, you can save money by purchasing finger-jointed molding, which is pieced together from short sections connected with zigzag joinery, or molding made of MDF.

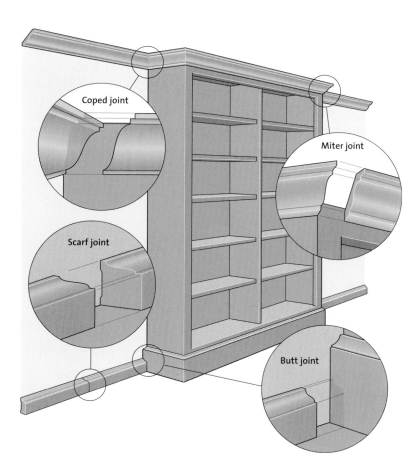

Coped joint

Scarf joint

Miter joint

Butt joint

Working with molding Some molding designs require only butt joints, which are relatively easy to make with basic tools. Other styles require miter joints, which are much trickier, especially if you will be using a clear finish and therefore can't cover up mistakes with caulk. If you face many miter joints and don't own a power miter saw, consider borrowing, buying, or renting one so you can nibble off short bits of wood until joints are perfect. Cutting consistently tight miters with a miter box and a backsaw takes far more skill.

There are four basic joints:

• A BUTT JOINT works well for molding that dead ends into a corner or against a wall. It's the simplest joint to make (see page 220).

• A SCARF JOINT connects pieces lengthwise. Cutting the ends with a saw set at an angle of about 30 degrees helps make the joint barely noticeable.

• A COPED JOINT is the best way to connect pieces when they meet at an inside corner (see opposite page).

• A MITER JOINT is the best option for outside corners (see page 221).

Making a coped joint

It's worth learning how to make coped joints, even though they take practice to master. Coped joints tend to remain tight regardless of the season, even when humidity fluctuations would be great enough to cause regular miter joints to open. Whenever possible, cut the coped joint before you trim the entire piece to its final length. That way, if you don't like the joint, you can try again.

On the most noticeable wall, usually the one you see when you first enter a room, install one piece of molding so it reaches all the way to the corner.

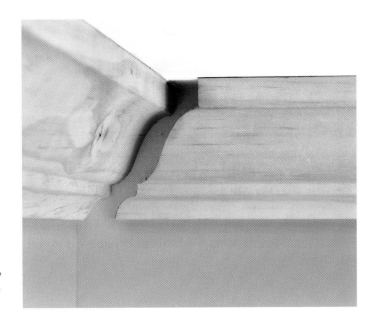

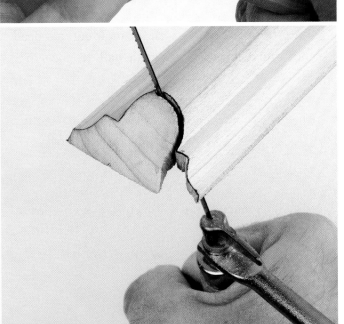

1 **MITER ONE END.** Cut the end of the least noticeable piece at a 45-degree angle, making the back edge longer than the front. Rub a pencil over the front edge so you can see it more easily.

2 **CUT AWAY EXCESS.** Hold a coping saw with the blade perpendicular to the molding, as if you were going to square-cut the end. Leave the pencil line as you cut the wood to create a mirror image of the molding's contour. Depending on the style of the molding you are cutting, you may need to scoot the blade out in the middle of the cut and come in from a different direction. When the cut is complete, test-fit the joint. To get a tight fit, you might need to remove small amounts of wood with a rasp or sandpaper.

Designing molding with butt joints

If you have only simple tools, avoid mitered joints by choosing molding that looks good with butt joints. Trim that extends in only one direction can have a fancy profile because all you need to do is cut the pieces to length. But if you have corners to turn, stick with flat pieces or purchase molding that is designed to be paired with special corner blocks, as shown below. Spark up the design by incorporating pieces of different widths and thicknesses.

When you are using flat molding and butt joints, little details can have a big impact. For example, the top piece of the frame around this built-in bookcase is thicker than the molding below it, and it's long enough to jut slightly beyond the vertical pieces. At the bottom of the frame, the verticals extend a short distance past a horizontal piece of the same width and thickness. Make the overhang at least 1/4 inch so it looks deliberate, not like sloppy work.

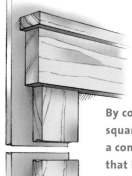

By combining pieces of flat or square trim, you can create a complex design for molding that incorporates only butt joints. A head cap (top left) can dress up molding across the top of a bookcase, while a plinth block (left) makes a nice anchor for built-ins that rest on the floor.

Basic butt joints create an elegant-looking frame around this built-in china cabinet, and they tie the piece to other woodwork in the room, such as the wainscot. The header extends past the sides, while the top trim on the wainscot includes a separate cap that's lined up with the bottom shelf of the cabinet.

By using corner blocks, you can install molding that turns a corner elegantly without mitering or coping. Choose blocks that are wide and thick enough to create equal reveals along the front and sides of the adjoining molding.

Making a miter joint

If you're working with a square corner and flat surfaces, making a clean miter can be as simple as cutting two pieces at a perfect 45-degree angle and nailing them to the wall. If you're using a power miter saw, its angle guide may be all the help you need. But corners aren't always square, and walls or other surfaces aren't always flat and plumb. Here are some tricks of the trade:

Use reveals Incorporate "reveals," the trim carpenter's term for setbacks, in your molding plan. The miter trim around this doorway, for example, is set about $\frac{1}{4}$ inch back from the door jamb. That setback gives you a little fudge factor when you are installing the trim, since your eye won't notice if the molding edge wanders slightly farther out or closer in.

Cut a test piece If you have a lot of trim to install, cut a short test piece with 45-degree angles on both ends. After you install each of the actual trim pieces, use the tester to check whether to cut the next piece at exactly a 45-degree angle, or one that is a little more or less sharp. If the tester is tight at the top but $\frac{1}{16}$ inch short on the bottom, for example, you could lightly draw a 45-degree line on the next piece of molding and adjust the saw so the blade touches that line at the top but leaves $\frac{1}{16}$ inch more wood at the bottom.

Measure accurately Once you miter one end of a piece of molding, it's sometimes difficult to figure out where to cut the other end. Instead of trying to hook your tape measure over the slanted edge, where it is prone to slide off, mark the length on a board with a square end. Align the short edge of the first miter with the end of the board, transfer the mark, and make the cut.

Shim the gap When two sides of a miter meet in a tight line but one sticks out farther than the other, insert a shim behind the piece that's recessed. Nail through the shim when you attach the molding to the wall. Use a sharp utility knife to trim the shim so it doesn't project past the molding. Cover the gap with caulk.

CREDITS

ILLUSTRATIONS

All illustrations by Greg Maxson, www.gregmaxson.com, unless otherwise noted.

T = top, B = bottom, L = left, R = right, M = middle

Beverley Bozarth Colgan: 66TL; Dartmouth Publishing and Tracy La Rue Hohn: 180BR, 180B, 187BR, 217BR; Tracy La Rue Hohn: 102BL, 104BR, 111TL, 141 all, 154BL; Bill Oetinger: 165 all, 180TL, 186 all, 187TL, 187M, 187TR, 197 all, 207 all 212 all, 216TR, 218BL; Rik Olson: 220 ML

PHOTOGRAPHS

All photographs by Chuck Kuhn unless otherwise noted.

T = top, B = bottom, L = left, R = right, M = middle

Abode/Beateworks/Corbis: 17TR, 31TL; Russell Abraham: 85BR; Jean Allsopp: 53TL, 53TR, 113BL, 127BL; Jean Allsopp & Laurey W. Glenn: 53BL, 53BR; Jean Allsopp & Rex Perry: 42TL, 42BR; Jean Allsopp & Harry Taylor: 126BL; Ralph Anderson: 43TL; David Ansley: 160BR; Michel Arnaud/Beateworks/Corbis: 69R; Scott Atkinson: 144BL, 145TR, 146BR, 146B, 148B, 149B, 152MR, 154TL, 154TR, 155TR, 158TL, 158BL, 161TL, 161MR, 162TR, 162BL, 163TR, 163BL, 168BM bottom row, 168BR bottom row, 168BL bottom row, 168BL top row, 168BM top row, 168BR top row, 217MR; Courtesy Avrack Inc.: 55TM; Patrick Barta/Corner House Photo Stock, Inc.: 87BR, 137BR; Carolyn Bates/Corner House Photo Stock, Inc,: 80TL; Fernando Bengoechea/Beateworks/Corbis: 35BR, 38T, 56TR, 136BL; Antoine Bootz & Jeff McNamara: 51TL; Andrew Bordwin/Beateworks/Corbis: 30TR, 31TR, 47BR; Botanica/Jupiter Images: 16TL; Brand X Pictures/Jupiter Images: 89T;

Jennifer Cheung/Botanica/Jupiter Images: 143BR; Corbis: 90, 91T, 93M, 94BL, 94BR, 95TR, 96TR, 96BR, 97BL, 99B, 101T, 102TR, 102BR, 103TL, 109BL, 110TR, 112B, 113TR, 114B, 115TL, 117B, 118BR, 119T, 119BL, 120BL, 121BL, 126BR, 128BL, 129BL, 130TL, 132TL, 133M, 133B; Corner House Photo Stock, Inc.: 91BL, 93B, 98BL, 100TR, 101BL, 101BR, 103BL, 103BR, 104TR, 106M, 109TL, 110BR, 114TR, 117TR, 121TR, 123BL, 133T; Steve Dubinsky: 116TR; Emeraldlight/Corbis: 77TL; Elizabeth Felicella/Beateworks/Corbis: 32BL; Scott Fitzgerrell: 219 all, 220BL; Dan Forer/Beateworks/Corbis: 17BL, 34TR, 39T, 51BL, 52BR; Morris Gindi/Corner House Photo Stock, Inc.: 13BR, 59TR; Laurey W. Glenn: 4BM, 20TR; Tria Govan: 99T, 127TL; Jay Graham/Corner House Photo Stock, Inc.: 26TR, 79BR, 85TL, 167BR, 203TR; John Granen: 59M, 62TR, 65BR, 100BL, 131BR, 131TR, 131BL, 142TR, 142B; Graphistock/Jupiter Images: 68TR; Jamie Hadley: 4TR, 8MR, 48, 68BR, 197TR, 197TL; Alex Hayden: 40T, 116BR; Douglas Hill/Beateworks/Corbis: 60BL, 152TL; Dana Hoff/Beateworks/Corbis: 37M, 85M; William Howard: 36R; Jeanne Huber: 143TR, 153MR, 175TL, 175ML, 175BMR; InsideOutPix/Jupiter Images: 17TL, 35BL; Douglas Johnson: 41TL, 115B; Richard Leo Johnson/Beateworks/Corbis: 63TL; Jupiter: 95BL, 119BR, 127TR, 129TR; Elliott Kaufman/Beateworks/Corbis: 39M, 50B, 70TR; Muffy Kibbey: 1, 4BL, 5BR, 10T, 11B, 13TL, 22B, 29BL, 65TL, 65BL, 72TL, 137T, 170TR, 174BL, 181BL, 202T; Courtesy Knape & Vogt Manufacturing Co.: 106T; Courtesy KraftMaid Cabinetry, Inc.: 40BR; Nancy

Lazarus/Beateworks/Corbis: 71BR; John Edward Linden/Beateworks/Corbis: 12TR; David Livingston: 120BR; Look Photography/Beateworks/Corbis: 57BR; Bob Manley/Corner House Photo Stock, Inc.: 21TL, 45BL, 59BL, 84BR, 220BR; Jeff McNamara: 79TL; Courtesy Merrilat: 138B, 140TR, 140BR; Daniel Nadelbach: 77B, 80BR, 83BR, 129TL; Olson Photographic/Corner House Photo Stock, Inc.: 14MR, 23BL, 23BR, 71MR, 76BL, 89BL; David Papazian/Beateworks/Corbis: 20BL; Courtesy Rev-a-Shelf, LLC: 203B; Ken Rice/Corner House Photo Stock, Inc.: 7TR, 8L, 15TL; Jo-Ann Richards/First Light/Jupiter Images: cover, 139BR, 139T; Eric Roth: 2T, 6BL, 6BR, 7TL, 8BR, 9TL, 13BL, 14TL, 14BR, 18TL, 18BR, 23T, 26TL, 27B, 28BR, 29T, 30BL, 32BR, 33TL, 33BL, 35TL, 35TR, 36TL, 36BL, 37BR, 41TR, 41BL, 44BL, 45BR, 46BL, 47TL, 50TL, 51TR, 52TR, 52MR, 54T, 54BL, 55TL, 55BL, 59TL, 59BR, 62MR, 66TR, 66BL, 67TR, 69BL, 74T, 75B, 82B, 83TL, 84BL, 86BL, 87BL, 88TL, 92T, 93T, 95TL, 95MR, 97T, 98BL, 104BL, 105TL, 105BL, 105BR, 106B, 107T, 107BL, 109TR, 111B, 113TL, 115MR, 118TR, 121TL, 121BR, 122T, 123TL, 123MR, 125TL, 125BL, 126TR, 129BR, 130BR, 143TL, 151, 170BL, 174BR, 192TL, 203TL; Andrea Rugg Photograph/Beateworks/Corbis: 15BR, 18BL, 19TL, 26BL, 60TR, 84TL, 89BR; Mark Rutherford: 134BM, 159TR, 159BL, 159BR, 163ML, 163MR, 188ML, 188BR, 189TL, 189MR, 198TL, 198ML, 198ML, 198BR, 198BL, 198MR, 200TL, 200MR, 200BL, 201ML, 201TR, 201MR, 201BR, 209MR, 211TR, 211MR, 211BR, 211BL, 211BM, 214MR, 214BL, 214BR, 215TR, 215ML, 215BMR, 215BR, 216ML,

216BL, 217TL, 217ML; Jamie Salomon/Corner House Photo Stock, Inc.: 45TR; Alan Shortall/Corner House Photo Stock, Inc.: 9B, 9TR, 12BL, 24TR, 24BR, 25B, 34B, 37TL, 39B, 44BR, 45Tl, 57BL, 71TL, 81, 81 inset, 146TR, 202BR; Thomas J. Story: 8TR, 33BR, 49BR, 60BR, 69B, 85TR, 87BR, 108BL, 117TL, 124TR, 137BL, 181TL; Tim Street-Porter: 71ML; Tim Street-Porter/Beateworks/Corbis: 7B, 31B, 47TR, 57T, 67B, 72BR, 73, 86TL, 88TR, 171TR; Bob Swanson: 58T; TonRo Image Stock/Jupiter Images: 61; Russell Underwood/Corbis: 62BL; Scott Van Dyke/Beateworks/Corbis: 47ML; Brian Vanden Brink: 63BR, 92BR; David Wakely: 15ML; Jessie Walker/Corner House Photo Stock, Inc.: 38BR; Phillip Wegener/Beateworks/Corbis: 18TR; Greg West/Corner House Photo Stock, Inc.: 69TL, 75T; Elizabeth Whiting & Associates/Corbis: 21B, 29BR, 47MR; Russ Widstrand/Corner House Photo Stock, Inc.: 48BM, 72TR; Michele Lee Willson, with styling by Laura Del Fava: 2BL, 4BR, 25TL, 25TR, 41BR, 48BL, 48BR, 53ML, 53MR, 78BR, 123MR, 124BL, 124BR, 165L; Courtesy Wood-Mode Custom Cabinetry: 203BR.

ARCHITECTS, CONTRACTORS, DESIGNERS

T = top, B = bottom, L = left, R = right, M = middle

Bainbridge Architect Collaborative: 100BL; Amy Baker Interior Design: 40T; Bay West Builders, baywestbuilders.com: 2BL, 4BR, 25TL, 25TR, 41BR, 48BL, 48BR, 53ML, 53MR, 78BR, 123MR, 124BR, 124BL, 164L; Brooks Interior Design: 4BM, 20TR; Bryan Byrnes Construction: 170TR; David Coleman: 124TR; Sam

DeSollar: 137T; **William Duff Architects, wdarch.com:** 2BL, 4BR, 25TL, 25TR, 41BR, 48BL, 48BR, 53ML, 53MR, 78BR, 123MR, 124BR, 124BL, 164L; **Folck West + Savage:** 126BL; **Fusch-Serold & Partners:** 51TL; **Steven Gambrel:** 99T, 127TL; **Karl Golden Architects:** 174BL; **Kate Halfon Creations:** 120BR; **Halperin & Christ:** 8MR; **Hansen & Associates Interiors:** 53BL, 53BR; **Henry Sprott Long & Associates:** 79TL; **Historical Concepts:** 43TL, 99T, 127TL; **Scott Johnson:** 71ML; **Cathy Kincaid Interiors:** 51TL; **Lake/Flato Architects, Inc.:** 53TL, 53TR, 127BL; **Lloyd Architects:** 8TR; **Looney Ricks Kiss Architects:** 4BM, 20TR; **Lovelace Interiors:** 53TL, 53TR, 127BL; **Sharon Low:** 8MR; **Stacey Mackey:** 174BL; **Mary Evelyn McKee Interiors:** 79TL; **Michael Meyer Fine Woodworking, mmfww.com:** 2BL, 4BR, 25TL, 25TR, 41BR, 48BL, 48BR, 53ML, 53MR, 78BR, 123MR, 124BR, 124BL, 164L; **Moberg Epstein Architects:** 131BR, 131TR, 131BL; **Timothy Murphy:** 137T; **Nevin Interior Design:** 43TL; **Gary Earl Parsons:** 170TR; **Pepe-Lunche Designs:** 202T; **Lindy Small Architecture:** 49BR, 60BR, 69B; **Kathryn Rogers Sogno Design Group:** 181BL; **Stone-Wood Design:** 15ML; **Summerour and Associates Architects:** 42TL, 42BR; **John Tee:** 53BL, 53BR; **Lane Williams Architect:** 40T; **Alison Wittaker Design:** 85BR; **Linda Woodrum:** 42TL, 42BR.

SPECIAL THANKS

The author would like to thank Bob Stanton, Stanton Specialties; David Beyl, Common Sense Woodworking; Frank Madera, Madera Woodworking, LLC; Kim Craig, KraftMaid Cabinetry; Greg Heuer, Architectural Woodwork Institute; Mike Muscardini; and Tom and Summer Starbuck. Thanks also to *Sunset* magazine.

RESOURCES

PAGES 16–17
National Gypsum Company
800-628-4662
www.nationalgypsum.com
High-Flex® drywall

Fypon
800-446-3040
www.fypon.com
Plastic niche inserts

Classic Details
803-356-4545
classicdetails.com

Architectural Products by Outwater
800-835-4400
www.outwater.com

Flex Molding Inc.
800-307-3357
www.flexiblemoulding.com
Curved or flexible molding

B. H. Davis Company
800-923-2771
www.curvedmouldings.com

PAGES 36–37
Rev-A-Shelf
800-626-1126
www.rev-a-shelf.com
Cabinet accessories

Knape & Vogt Manufacturing Co.
www.knapeandvogt.com

Richelieu Hardware
800 253-1561
www.richelieu.com

Woodfold-Marco Mfg Inc.
503-357-7181
www.woodfold.com
Bookshelf doors

PAGES 38–39
Enkeboll Designs
800-745-5507
www.enkeboll.com
Carved overlays

Castlewood
800-346-4042
www.castlewood.com

PAGES 40–41
White River Hardwoods
800-558-0119
www.whiteriver.com
Cabinet feet

PAGES 46–47
Pegasus Associates Lighting
800-392-4818
www.pegasusassociates.com
Cabinet lighting

Phantom Lighting Systems
800-863-1184
www.phantomlighting.com

PAGES 56–57
Putnam Rolling Ladder Co.
212-226-5147
www.putnamrollingladder.com
Rolling library ladder

PAGES 142–143
Scherr's Cabinet and Doors
701-839-3384
www.scherrs.com
Cabinet components

Drawer Box Specialties
800-422-9881
www.dbsdrawers.com

Western Dovetail Inc.
800-800-3683
www.westerndovetail.com

Top Drawer Components
800-745-9540
www.topdrwr.com

Drawer Connection, Inc.
877-917-4887
www.dcdrawers.com

Wholesale Cabinet Doors
951-681-9429
www.wholesalecabinetdooors.com

PAGES 172–173
Woodcraft
800-225-1153
www.woodcraft.com
Double-stick tape

PAGES 190–191
Headcote Smart-Bit
800-443-7937
www.mcfeelys.com
Countersink bit

INDEX